Vatican II:
The Liturgy
Constitution

EDITOR

Austin Flannery, O.P.

SCEPTER BOOKS, DUBLIN

First edition April 1964

Second edition July 1964

Third edition November 1964

PRINTED IN THE REPUBLIC OF IRELAND

This book is based on commentaries published in the February 1964 issue of *Doctrine and Life*. It is set on 10 on 11 pt New Times Roman and printed for Scepter Publishers Ltd, 144 Lower Baggot Street, Dublin 2 by the Leinster Leader Ltd, Naas, Co. Kildare, Ireland. *Nihil Obstat:* Patricius Harris, *Censor Deputatus. Imprimatur:* Thomas, *Ep. Darensis et Leighlinensis.* 14.11.64.

Contents

Contributors

FATHER AUSTIN FLANNERY, O.P., is Editor of *Doctrine and Life*.

FATHER PIERRE-MARIE GY, O.P., is assistant director of the *Institut Supérieur de Liturgie*, Paris, and professor of theology at the Saulchoir, France. He was a consultor to the pre-conciliar commission on the liturgy.

FATHER COLMAN O'NEILL, O.P., is professor of dogmatic theology at Fribourg University, Switzerland.

FATHER MICHAEL MYERSCOUGH, C.P., is professor of liturgy at the Passionist House of Studies, Consett, Co Durham, England.

FATHER LIAM WALSH, O.P., is professor of liturgy at the Dominican House of Studies, Tallaght, Co Dublin, Ireland.

FATHER VINCENT RYAN, O.S.B., is professor of liturgy at St Columba's Abbey, Glenstal, Co Limerick, Ireland.

FATHER KIERAN O'GORMAN is director of sacred music in the diocese of Killaloe, Ireland.

FATHER DONAL O'SULLIVAN, S.J., is chairman of the Arts Council of Ireland.

MOST REVEREND JOSEPH RODGERS, D.D., is the Bishop of Killaloe, Ireland.

WILFRID CANTWELL is Vice-President of the Royal Institute of the Architects of Ireland.

Foreword

The Constitution on the Sacred Liturgy came into force on 16 February 1964. Its implementation is, to a great extent, a long-term programme. It is a very delicate undertaking, which, as Pope Paul VI insists, must needs be left to the judgment of those who have competence and authority in this sphere. The Constitution itself has defined who the authorities are to whose care the programme is committed.

In the meantime, however, and side-by-side with this work of implementation, there is a work which all priests, brothers, nuns and layfolk – each in his own measure – must undertake. It is a work of study. The obligation lies especially on the clergy. Father Ferdinand Antonelli, o.f.m., secretary of the liturgical commission, said, in an article in the *Osservatore Romano* (8 December, 1963): 'What is needed, now, is that the clergy who have the care of souls should endeavour at once to enter into the spirit of the Constitution, in order to communicate it subsequently to their people'.

The Constitution is, in part, the product of some forty years of study and experience of liturgical renewal. A full understanding of it presupposes a liturgical awareness which has not been widely distributed in the Church hitherto, but has tended to be confined to those who have kept closely in touch with the liturgical movement. Many people, one feels, will find gaps in their knowledge which will make it difficult for them, at times, to perceive the full import of the Constitution. It was here, we felt, that people of special competence, who had been in touch with the liturgical movement for some years, could be of some assistance. We invited six of them to divide the Constitution between them, each of them taking the sections in which he was most competent. We asked them to fill the gaps, as it were, providing the liturgical or theological context which the Constitution presupposes and in which its significance is perceived more fully. We are also reproducing an article from one of the great liturgical journals, *La Maison Dieu*. It is by Father Pierre Marie Gy, o.p., and it describes the drawing up of the Constitution as well as the fashioning of the milieu—the liturgical movement—which helped to shape it. We are grateful to Father Gy, o.p. and to Father A.-M. Roguet, o.p., editor of *La Maison Dieu*, for giving us permission to reproduce Father Gy's article from that journal.

The translation of the Constitution itself was made by the Most Reverend Dr Thomas Rodgers, the Bishop of Killaloe and was first published in the *Irish Ecclesiastical Record*. We are most grateful to Dr Rodgers, to the editor of the *Irish Ecclesiastical Record* and to Messrs Browne and Nolan, Dublin for permission to use His Lordship's translation.

New material in the second edition of this book included the original text, translation and a commentary on the new decree of the Sacred Congregation of Rites on the formula for distributing Holy Communion; and pronouncements of the hierarchies of Ireland, of England and Wales and of the United States regarding the implementation of the Constitution. The bibliography was enlarged to include new texts on the subject.

The need to publish a third edition is, we feel, indicative of the wide use being made of this book by those officially concerned with implementing the Constitution and by clergy and laity alike. It is particularly gratifying to learn that it has become a text in certain theology faculties. The present edition contains, in addition to material published in previous editions, a full translation of the new *Instructio* by the Sacred Congregation of Rites: this important document is in fact a commentary on the Constitution, giving authoritative directives on its implementation.

The fifth chapter of the *Instructio* contains directives on church building. The directives are clear and simple, but we felt that, for many of our readers their meaning could be perceived even more clearly with the help of illustrations. For this reason we invited Mr Wilfrid Cantwell, an architect, to devise plans and perspective drawings to illustrate what is meant by chapter five.

AUSTIN FLANNERY, O.P.

Promulgation[1]

POPE PAUL VI

The arduous and complex debates have not been without fruit. The discussion of one of the themes, that of the sacred liturgy, has been brought to a satisfactory conclusion. The liturgy was the first subject to be examined and the first too, in a sense, in intrinsic worth and in importance for the life of the Church. We have solemnly promulgated the Constitution on the Sacred Liturgy this day.

This is a source of considerable satisfaction to Us. We note in the Constitution a respect for the hierarchy of values and of duties. God, in the first place; prayer, our first duty; the liturgy, the first source of the divine life which is given to us, the first school of the spiritual life, the first gift which is ours to give to the Christian people who pray with us and share our beliefs; the first invitation to the world to loosen, in true and blessed prayer, its mute tongue, to feel the ineffable regenerative power of chanting with us the praise of God and the hopes of men, through Christ Our Lord and in the Holy Spirit.

We cannot pass over in silence the careful observance of the liturgy by the faithful of the oriental rites: may they always hold it as a school of truth and may it be for them a flame of love.

It will be well for us to treasure this fruit of our Council: it should animate and characterize the life of the Church. The Church is a religious society, a community of prayer, it is a people amongst whom the interior life, the life of the spirit, is made to flourish by faith and grace.

If, at this juncture, we have set out to simplify the external expression of worship, in an effort to make it more comprehensible to our people and closer to current speech, this does not mean that we wish to reduce the importance of prayer, or to put it on a lower plane than

1. An extract from the address by Pope Paul VI at the close of the second session of the Vatican Council, 4 December, 1962. The translation is by Father Austin Flannery, O.P.

other obligations of the sacred ministry or of the apostolate. Neither does it mean that we want to make worship less expressive or less aesthetically satisfying. It is rather that we want to make it purer, more genuine, closer to the sources of truth and grace, better fitted to be the spiritual patrimony of the people.

To ensure that this will be so, we desire that nobody will meddle with the rules governing the official prayer of the Church, introducing private reforms or special rites; that nobody will claim the right to anticipate arbitrarily the application of the Constitution which We have promulgated today. All must wait until opportune and authoritative instructions will have been issued, and they must await the approval of the reforms which the post-conciliar commissions will prepare.

The nobility of the Church's prayer lies in its harmony throughout the world. Let no man disturb it, let no man meddle with it.

(*Osservatore Romano*, 5 December, 1963)

The constitution in the making[1]

PIERRE MARIE GY, O.P.

Some time after he had announced his intention of calling an ecumenical council, the late Pope John XXIII entrusted its preparation to three secretariats and eleven commissions. Of these, the liturgical commission faced problems which were posed quite differently from those which most of the other commissions encountered. These other commissions – and the Catholic world at large – began to be aware of problems which up to then had not been adequately formulated. It was only after the announcement of the conciliar *aggiornamento* and the enquiry addressed to the bishops that the Church began actively to consider them, thus, in many instances, bringing them rapidly to a head. The problem of the reform of the liturgy, on the other hand, had already come to a head. The need for an over-all decision had become imperative, a decision by an energetic pope or . . . by a council.

THE RENEWAL OF THE LITURGY

A programme of liturgical reform had been developing for a number of years, as readers of the liturgical reviews, such as *La Maison Dieu*, will know. Did it originate with Pius XII's decision to establish a commission for the complete overhauling of the liturgy – a decision re-echoed by *Ephemerides Liturgicae* from 1948 – or with the spread of the liturgical apostolate throughout the world? Without doubt it owed its origin to a combination of the two: the visible head of the Church and the whole body, each giving the appropriate response and support to the other. Everything conspired to the same end: there were the echoes awakened by the reforms of Pius XII, even in countries where the liturgical apostolate had scarcely penetrated; the gradual realization by pastors of souls that the liturgical apostolate must needs have repercussions on the very structure of the liturgy; the celebration of the liturgy in missionary contexts, whether in the dechristianized West or the newly evangelized civilizations; the influence of certain great national liturgical centres and the role

1. Reprinted from *La Maison Dieu*, No 76 (No 4 of 1963) by kind permission of the author and the editor. The translation is by Father Austin Flannery, o.p.

of the principal members of the Roman commission for reform – Father Ferdinand Antonelli, O.F.M., of the Congregation of Rites, Father (now Cardinal) Augustine Bea, S..J, then private confessor to Pope Pius XII and intermediary between the commission and the Pope, Father G. Löw, prolific author, who died on the eve of the Council; the reception given by the pope of *Mediator Dei* to the representations made to him by the hierarchies of Germany, France and elsewhere, even though it is likely that his personal piety inclined him in a different direction.

Four points, especially, came increasingly to the fore: the pastoral character of the liturgy; its importance for the missions; the necessity of introducing the living languages into the liturgy; the desire for concelebration.

One after another, the different countries came into contact with the liturgical apostolate. Some people, taking their stand on the difficulty of translation, argued that, side by side with the pastoral liturgy, there was a whole section of the liturgy which had no need of being pastoral. Gradually, however, the conviction spread through the Church that the liturgy was wholly and intrinsically pastoral. The Assisi Congress (1956) and the *Instruction* issued in 1958 were, in this respect, decisive steps in the direction of the conciliar constitution. The conviction was gaining ground that it is in its entirety that the liturgy is pastoral.

At the Assisi congress, especially, it became clear that the liturgical movement had ceased to be confined to a small number of countries and had taken on the dimensions of the Church. This was particularly noticeable in the missionary countries where – thanks to the wide-ranging apostolate of Father Hofinger, the zeal of several bishops and the congresses of Nijmegen and Eichstätt – it began to be accepted that missionary endeavour must needs include the liturgical apostolate.

However, as the liturgical movement spread and as reform succeeded reform, it began to appear that insurmountable obstacles stood in the way of the most important reforms. This was the case with the central question of the language of the liturgy. It is true that bilingual rituals were multiplying and that the privilege of the 'German High Mass',[2] for all that it came under fire several times, was in every instance confirmed and, indeed, was conceded to missionary bishops with little difficulty. But, at the same time, the

2. The 'German High Mass' consists of a Sung Mass during which the faithful sing vernacular hymns in place of the Creed, etc. It was approved by Rome in 1943 (Translator).

reading of the epistle and gospel of the Mass by the priest in the vernacular was excluded, or, rather, the decision was left by Pius XII to another pontificate.

It was the same with the question of restoring concelebration. It seems probable that this was seriously considered for Holy Thursday in 1955, it is certain that it was considered in 1957 for the centenary celebrations at Lourdes. However, to make it feasible, it was necessary to settle certain theological controversies and to give a larger dimension to the kind of priestly eucharistic piety which saw concelebration as a pointless and disturbing innovation. Pius XII clearly found the proposal tempting and he set himself to clarify the doctrinal basis for concelebration in his discourse to the members of the Assisi congress and in a reply by the Holy Office.[3] However, just when concelebration had become a practical possibility, the idea was abandoned.

THE INTERNATIONAL LITURGICAL CONGRESSES

The liturgical reform (and people's understanding of the liturgy) progressed constantly in some sectors and not at all in others, but it received support and inspiration from the international meetings which took place every year from 1950. In 1950, it is true, only France and Germany took part, but from 1951 the meetings were truly international. Some of them were confined to experts, leading liturgists from the different countries, others were widened to the proportions of congresses. A close liaison was established with the pontifical commission for reform from 1952, and from 1953 its principal members took part successively in the meetings.

One can realize, after the event, the importance of the contacts established between different countries during these years, the usefulness of the collaboration effected and of the work accomplished. Many problems were examined and brought to a head as a result of the discussions which took place at these meetings, from 1950 to 1960, and of the studies undertaken in connection with them. Simultaneously, there developed a widespread desire to see them solved. At the same time, the meetings created a milieu in which many people shared the same pastoral and informed understanding of the liturgy and gained experience of working together.

3. Text of Pope Pius's discourse in *The Furrow*, 1956, Oct. and Nov; *Irish Ecclesiastical Record*, 1956, pp. 344 ff; *Worship*, 1956, Dec., pp. 48 ff. Text of reply of Holy Office in *AAS*, 1957 p. 370. (Translator).

THE PRE-CONCILIAR COMMISSION

It would seem natural to look to that milieu when staffing the pre-conciliar commission on the liturgy, but it might well be objected that to do so would be to pre-judge the problem of the reform. And, in fact, French and German bishops and the directors of the national liturgical centres, Trier and Paris, were at first excluded. However, it soon became obvious that their help was needed. The following were, in consequence, co-opted on to the commission and played an important part on it: Mgr H. Jenny, auxiliary bishop of Cambrai, France, Mgr O. Spuelbeck, apostolic administrator of Meissen, East Germany, Fathers A.-M. Roguet, o.p. and A. G. Martimort, co-directors of the Centre of Pastoral Liturgy, Paris, Mgr J. Wagner, director of the Liturgical Institute at Trier, Germany.

For the rest, under the authority of its president, Cardinal Gaetano Cicognani, the recruitment of the members of the commission was carried out in obedience to two criteria: that of securing the services of the most effective and competent men, and that of ensuring an equable representation of the different parts of the Church – continents, countries, religious orders. Some people complained that this second criterion was insufficiently observed.

One ought to mention here that Father A. Bugnini, an Italian Vincentian, was a happy choice as secretary. He had been secretary of the commission for reform set up by Pius XII. He was a gifted organiser and possessed an open-minded, pastoral spirit. Many people noted how, with Cardinal Cicognani, he was able to imbue the discussions with the liberty of spirit recommended by Pope John XXIII.

THE PREPARATION OF THE SCHEMA

Father Bugnini has described the work of the commission in an article written for the *Osservatore Romano* (1 April, 1962). The work was divided among sub-committees, each of them devoting four months of intensive work to one of the thirteen sections of the schema: the liturgical mystery, liturgical formation, active participation, liturgical language, adaptation (chapter one); the Mass, concelebration (chapter two); the sacraments (chapter three); the divine office (chapter four); sacred music (chapter six); sacred art, vestments and furniture (chapter seven); the calendar (appendix). There was a certain amount of repetition, it was found. Thus, the problem of the language of the liturgy cropped up in different sections, and in the end, a special chapter on the liturgical year was added. There was at least one bishop on every sub-committee, but he did not take charge.

The texts composed by the sub-committees took their places in the complete schema, which was examined in its entirety three times: in the session held in April 1961, again by means of a written consultation and, finally, in the session held in January 1962.

The commission had to prepare a conciliar document, an undertaking of which none of its members had had previous experience. It was a task for which – and all the pre-conciliar commissions had a similar experience – liturgical or theological competence do not suffice, nor is any specialized knowledge of much avail. What is needed is a minimum of knowledge of the great Councils, a broad outlook and a certain intuitive awareness of the signs of the times.

There were two preliminary problems, on whose solution most of the rest of the work would depend. Should the document confine itself to the Latin liturgy? Should it be practical, containing only decisions on reform, or should these be afforded a theological justification?

The first question was indeed a very important one: the Council was not to be a Council of the Latin Church, but an Ecumenical Council. Was it right that the preparatory commission should confine itself to the Latin liturgy? Further, one has not properly posed the problem of the language of the Latin liturgy unless one has situated the Latin Church in the totality of the *Catholica*. On the other hand, in most of the Oriental Churches, the problem of reform, urgent as it might be, cannot be examined seriously save in the context of dialogue between the Churches which are in communion with Rome and those which are not. It was necessary, therefore, to leave this question aside, to treat only of the reform of the Roman liturgy, referring, as need arose, to examples from the Oriental Churches (in the case of concelebration, for example), eventually enunciating principles whose validity would not be limited to the Western liturgy.

The solution of the second problem was obvious at once: the document ought to be at once disciplinary and doctrinal. In conciliar categories, it ought to be, not a simple decree, but a constitution. In this connection one can only regret that the pre-conciliar ruling on mixed commissions did not operate so as to permit collaboration with the theological commission.

Once it had been decided to prepare a schema which would be at once doctrinal and practical, the next thing was to discover, gradually, the style that was appropriate to it. According to the tradition of the Council of Trent and even of Vatican I, it should be biblical and patristic, and should maintain a certain distance from theological disputes. But should one not, at the same time, take account of the doctrinal style of the encyclicals, which are more concerned with theological precisions and are somewhat removed from biblical theology? The question was all the more relevant since Pius XII had devoted considerable attention to the liturgy, in the encyclical, *Mediator Dei*, and elsewhere. Should the conciliar constitution be a solemn prolongation of the Pope's teaching? Could it conceivably abstract from it?

Little by little a delicate solution emerged, a solution which seems to have pleased the Council Fathers and to have inspired even the theological commission in its revision of schemas. The style of the Constitution, it was decided, would be that traditionally adopted in Councils; it would be wholly biblical, except where canonical precision was necessary. Thus it is that the opening pages, on the history of salvation, are closer to biblical theology than to the style of *Mediator Dei*. However, at the same time, the Constitution relies considerably on the great encyclical of Pius XII and time and again it uses its very terminology, without quotation marks or reference. Only in the case of biblical, liturgical and patristic quotations are references given.

One problem that arose was whether or not the schema should enter into details. In certain cases it was obviously desirable to have a programme of reform precise enough to be sure of implementation. If the formulation of the Council's proposal was too vague, one would risk giving the conciliar fathers the impression that they were being asked to issue *carte blanche* in the matter of liturgical reform. On the other hand, a detailed programme of reform was not worthy of an ecumenical council nor in keeping with its role. The result, in fact, was a schema which outlined the principles of reform, what John XXIII called, *apropos* of the breviary, 'the higher principles, *altiora principia*', the schema itself, however, being accompanied by *Declarationes*, an explanatory commentary destined for the conciliar fathers. During the conciliar debates of October and November 1962, there were several complaints that the *Declarationes* had not been distributed. At length this omission was remedied in part. The *Declarationes* are the base of the schema, it is they which give it its density. They are like the lower part of an iceberg, the most important part, for all that it remains hidden under the water. However, the *Declarationes* are not in any sense binding on the post-conciliar commission.

THE SCHEMA IS PRESENTED IN THE COUNCIL

The schema prepared by the liturgical commission was given its definitive shape and was accepted by a plenary session in a vote taken on 13 January, 1962. Duplicated copies were at once made, for transmission to the central commission. The programme of reform was so vast that it caused the president, Cardinal Gaetano Cicognani, to hesitate; he waited a week and signed the document on 1 February. He died on 5 February.

Cardinal Cicognani's successor was appointed on 22 February, he was Cardinal Larraona. That same day the Holy Father promulgated the Constitution, *Veterum Sapientia*, which, among other prescriptions, forbade any attack on the use of Latin in the liturgy. Subsequently, the schema was discussed by the central commission, in which the balance of tendencies was very different from what it was to be in the Council. The schema was later subjected to restrictive changes. Father Bugnini, who had shared the helm with the late Cardinal Cicognani, lost his chair at the Lateran and was not made secretary of the conciliar commission subsequently.

The Council began on 11 October, 1962 and the Fathers set about electing the members of the conciliar commissions. Six of the bishops elected to the liturgical commission had belonged to the preconciliar liturgical commission. Amongst others, one must single out Cardinal Giacomo Lercaro, who for years had been one of the leaders of the liturgical movement, and Mgr. G. Van Bekkum, the spokesman for the liturgy of the missions. The secretary of the commission was Father Ferdinand Antonelli, o.f.m., who had figured prominently on the commission for reform set up by Pius XII.

THE DEBATE ON THE SCHEMA

The debate on the schema occupied fifteen general congregations (22 October to 13 November). The debate was badly organized, but it was extremely useful, even when it was long-drawn and repetitious.[4] It gave a chance to the Fathers who were not fully abreast of developments to inform themselves and make up their minds on the general problems put by the schema (doctrinal style of the Council, role of the bishops' conferences) and on the reform of the liturgy itself. The Council not merely revealed a common denominator pre-existent among the bishops, it quickly enough created a new one. Public

4. There were 328 oral interventions (Cardinal Ruffini, 6 times; Cardinals Léger and Spellman, 4 times each) and more than 350 written interventions.

debate revealed the true worth of authorities and arguments. Above all, in spite of the diversity of situations within the Church, there was agreement on the necessity of reform. The young Churches and Latin America went further in their demands for vernacular liturgy and adaptation than did the preconciliar commission. Once again, the question of liturgical language was central to these debates. It is likely that there is no argument, pro or contra, of any weight or worth, which was not heard in St Peter's during those days.

Among the questions which were most in the forefront of the debate, that of communion under both kinds met particular opposition. One wonders if that part of the Constitution would have been passed if it had been put to a separate vote.

On the question of the reform of the divine office, the majority – which was apparent enough after the debate had commenced – was divided between a multitude of contradictory opinions. One had here, as was evident during the preparation of the schema, a question almost as difficult as that of the language of the liturgy. The reason for this was a certain tension inherent in Christian prayer, especially in the prayer of the apostle, and caused by the absence of the absolute criteria afforded by the divine institution in other parts of the liturgy.[5] It may also be caused by the illusions or the hypocrisy which have often accumulated in this domain.

Lastly, it is to be noted that while sacred music is of considerable importance – and, indeed, some people wanted to give it a central place in the schema – it attracted little attention in the Council.

APPROVAL AND AMENDMENTS

On 14 November, the Council gave massive approval, in principle, to the schema on the liturgy (2162 *placet*, 46 *non placet*). It remained for the conciliar commission – which set to work slowly at first, picking up speed as it went on – to analyse the written text of all the interventions by the Fathers, extracting from them the amendments the Council desired. This enormous task was completed, with regard to the Introduction and the first chapter (one-third of the Constitution), in about a month. The amendments to Articles 1 to 46 were voted on between 17 November and 6 December, 1962. The revision of the Constitution was completed between the two sessions

5. Thus, since Christ instituted the sacraments and, in several of them, gave very precise directives, we are in possession of absolute standards of judgment in that domain; not so, however, with regard to the divine office. (Translator).

and the remaining amendments were voted on during the second session.

Each chapter was submitted to a final vote, the terms being: *placet, placet juxta modum*, or *non placet*, the *placet juxta modum* being counted with the *placets*. It was the task of the commission, however, to take back to the Council Fathers the results of its deliberations on the *modi* – the desired amendments. It was the opinion of all that it did this with extreme fidelity. In two cases, especially, for the Mass (781 votes *juxta modum*) and for the sacraments (1,054 votes *juxta modum*), the commission thought it best to present new amendments, which gave to the ordinary of the place (*ordinarius loci*) a general control over concelebration in his diocese, and submitting, without restriction, the choice of the language of the sacraments to episcopal conferences. The voting took place on 22 November.

If one considers the amendments to the Constitution as a whole, including those added while the *modi* (i.e. changes suggested by Fathers who voted *placet juxta modum*) were being examined, a large number of them will be seen to concern particular points which were either reinforced or softened, or were clarified and made more precise. Two classes of amendment, however, are worthy of mention. One class concerns doctrine and, ultimately, doctrinal continuity between Vatican II and Trent; the other class concerns the use of the vernacular at present and for the future.

If, from the point of view of ecclesiology, Vatican II corresponds, in a sense, with Vatican I and complements it, from the point of view of the theology of the liturgy and of the sacraments – and of the whole attitude to liturgical reform – it is with Trent that comparison seems relevant. At the present time, certainly, there is no need for the Catholic Church to remain on the defensive, to be content to affirm what the reformers questioned. The Church owes it to the faithful – and, ultimately, to Our Lord – to resume all that is evangelically valid in the liturgical perceptions of the reformers. The observers at the Council have rightly emphasized this aspect of the Council's achievement. On the other hand, however, the Church must assert her teaching's accord with earlier Councils, and the complete homogeneity of the faith. A number of amendments inserted at the behest of the Fathers – several of them referring to the sacrificial character of the Eucharist – served to underline this last point.

During the debates and the voting on the language of the liturgy, the Council, with its pastoral bias, showed that there was no justification for the vicissitudes suffered by the schema in the Spring and Summer of 1962. In the council chamber, it won the assent of an assembly, some of whose members favoured more conservative, and others more advanced, measures than those outlined in the text of the schema. It was obvious, however, that an Ecumenical Council must do more than meet the needs of the present; it must also foresee future developments and must shape them. It must make provision for an increasing use of the vernacular, for new adaptations and, even, for the emergence of new liturgical rites over and above those now in use in East and West. Too radical a change would be a pastoral evil. At the same time, the Council must guide, pastorally, today's and tomorrow's progressive evolution.

Pope Paul VI, who presided over the second session of the Council, was one of those who, on 22 October, 1962, on the first day of the debate, gave the schema his support. When, as head of the Church, he promulgated the Constitution on 4 December, 1964, he underlined the importance of the liturgy: 'the first to be examined and the first, too, in a sense, by reason of its intrinsic value and its importance in the life of the Church'.

Introduction and Chapter One

General Principles

COLMAN O'NEILL, O.P.

In conformity with the stated aims of the Council, the *Constitution on the Sacred Liturgy* is primarily a pastoral document. It is concerned, that is to say, with the broad principles which are to govern the adaptation of the liturgy so that it may become again what it once was, and what it is meant to be: a form of worship and sanctification which genuinely corresponds to the needs of Christians. This first published result of the Council's discussions may be fairly assessed and accurately interpreted only in these practical perspectives.

That some form of adaptation of the liturgy was called for has been clear for some time to those whose duty in the Church brings them into immediate contact with large groups of the faithful. The Council has shown itself to be thoroughly aware of the difficulties of the parish priest who wants to see his people taking part with appreciation and profit in the Mass and the celebration of the sacraments.

And it has got to the heart of the matter in a quite remarkable way·
With a deft and sure hand it has laid bare the central reality of the
liturgy, separating what is essential from what is the product of two
thousand years of history, and has gone on to formulate practical
norms, derived from what is central and essential and orientated by
pastoral experience.

Pastors and laity who have grasped the meaning and importance
of the liturgy can only rejoice at the clear and penetrating directives
laid down by the Council. The same may be said for theologians;
for the theologian too is concerned with the practical consequences
of his science; and in this Constitution he can find concrete expression, in the form of laws governing the practice of every Catholic
church in the world, given to some of the most profound truths of
the Christian faith. It is not always that the contemplative can see
the ideas to which he is committed being realized in action. Could
this happen, at least on such a scale, anywhere but in the Church of
Christ?

In order to achieve what may, without exaggeration, be called a
masterpiece of legislation, the Council had to refer to the nature of
the liturgy as it has been revealed; for the Church is never, and
cannot be, merely pragmatic. In harmony with their aim, the conciliar Fathers have sought out and proclaimed with almost painful,
certainly dramatic, single-mindedness, the inner reality of the liturgy.
God, working through Christ, active in the Church, saving mankind,
is there. His activity takes shape in the Church in word and ritual.
Men must discover him there and open themselves to him. And to
do this they must understand the words and ritual and be able to
adopt them as the natural expression of their own desire for God.

This approach seeks the significance of the liturgy by adopting the
method which the First Vatican Council described as discovering the
connection which exists between the various revealed mysteries. It is
one of the processes of theology. The theologian must prepare for
it, and complement it, with analysis of each detail of the mysteries.
And here a note of warning must be sounded. Because analysis is
so essential a part of his science there is the possibility that the
professional theologian will be disappointed with the *Constitution on
Liturgy;* for only vestigial traces of the analytic process appear there.
To entertain such disappointment would be to misunderstand the
purpose of the present Council. Lack of emphasis on the analytic
element of theology certainly characterizes the reported discussions
of conciliar problems. But, it must be remembered, the conciliar
Fathers deliberately chose a mode of procedure adapted to Chris-

tianity in the mid-twentieth century. The present circumstances of the Church require a return to essentials, to sources, to the breathtaking simplicity of the complex design of God for bringing his people to himself. Because it follows this line the *Constitution on Liturgy* presents a more dramatic form of teaching than that proposed by Pius XII in his encyclical letter, *Mediator Dei;* but this encyclical will nevertheless remain the basic authoritative analysis of the liturgy. On several points the encyclical is more explicit and more developed theologically than the Constitution. In particular there springs to mind Pius XII's noteworthy teaching on the baptismal character and on the participation of the faithful in the Mass.

The success of the Constitution on the liturgy is assured. Principally a pastoral Council, Vatican II has produced an enlightened revision of legislation that is unparalleled in Church history. It was guided by a vision of the essentials of the liturgical mystery. The way it formulates these essentials is striking and forceful.

INTRODUCTION

Three brief articles which serve as Introduction to the Constitution indicate the importance, within the context of the Council's aims, of discussing the liturgy. The second article is noteworthy for the concise and profound description it gives of the Church.

Art. 2. Anticipating what is to be explained more fully in Chapter One, the article states that in the liturgy, particularly in the Mass, 'the work of our redemption is carried forward';[1] and for this reason its celebration serves to express and to display to others both the mystery of Christ and the authentic nature of the true Church. That it gives expression to the mystery of Christ is clear, for the liturgy *is* part of the mystery of Christian redemption being realized in the world today. For this very reason the liturgy also manifests the true nature of the Church, since the Church is nothing else than the place in which the mystery of redemption is being realized. The liturgy is the most characteristic and the most efficacious activity of the Church; and the qualities which are to be found in the liturgy are the qualities which belong to the Church. To both may be applied, consequently, the description which is given to the latter:

1. The text used in the preparation of this commentary was the Latin original, published with a German translation commissioned by the German, Austrian, and Swiss bishops (Rome 1963). Subsequently, English translations have been largely brought into conformity with the translation prepared by Father C. Howell, s.j. (Cirencester 1963).

It is of the essence of the Church that she be both human and divine, visible and yet endowed with invisible realities, eager to act and yet intent on contemplation, present in this world and yet not at home in it; and she is all these things in such wise that in her the human is directed and subordinated to the divine, the visible likewise to the invisible, action to contemplation, and this present world to that city yet to come, which we seek.

Not only, then, does the liturgy build up the mystical body of those who already belong to Christ; it also serves, as a natural consequence of this, to bring the Church before the eyes of the world as the living mystery of Christian salvation.

CHAPTER ONE

GENERAL PRINCIPLES

The chapter, as its title indicates, deals with the general principles which are to govern the restoration, or adaptation, and the promotion of the liturgy. The text of the Constitution itself is divided into four principal sections; but, in harmony with the themes discussed, the chapter may be divided, for the sake of simplicity, into the following two parts with their sub-divisions:

I (a) The nature of the liturgy.
  (b) Its importance in the life of the Church.
II Promotion of the faithful's participation.
  (a) The faithful's participation.
  (b) Instruction of the clergy.
  (c) Adaptation of the text and ritual.
  (d) Liturgical significance of the diocese and parish.
  (e) Promotion of the pastoral-liturgical movement.

I (a) THE NATURE OF THE LITURGY (Arts. 5 – 8).

Art. 5. Salvation is seen under its fundamental aspect as a divine initiative which takes definitive form in the mission of the Word in the Incarnation. This mission was foreshadowed in God's care for his people in the Old Testament and its potentialities are fulfilled in the Church.

The humanity of Christ, united to the divine Word, was accordingly the instrument of our salvation, so that in Christ 'the perfect

achievement of our reconciliation came forth, and the fullness of
divine worship was given to us'. The two-fold significance which is
here indicated in Christ's earthly mission is to be discovered principally in his Passion, Resurrection and Ascension. These three events
form the single Paschal Mystery, so called because it was the fulfilment by Christ in the history of mankind's salvation of the Exodus
of the Israelites from captivity and of the Jewish paschal liturgy
which commemorated that divine saving action.

In this supreme mystery Christ 'dying, destroyed our death and
rising, restored our life'. The traditional image of the Church issuing
from the side of the crucified Christ expresses the truth that Christ's
death and resurrection are effective for us only through the ministra-
tions of the Church. For this reason the Church is called a 'sacrament' or a 'mystery' (both words translate *sacramentum*); for it is the
visible presence in the world of the ever-active central mystery of
Christ's Pasch; and through the visible actions of the Church Christ's
Pasch effectively saves individual men.

Art. 6. The metaphorical description of the Church as issuing
from the side of the dying Christ is now reduced to more literal and
more explicit terms; in this process the place of the liturgy in the
Church is more clearly defined.

Being sent by Christ and being filled with the Holy Spirit, the
apostles shared in the mission from the Father of the Word made
flesh. Their function in the Church was firstly one of preaching the
Gospel of salvation through Christ; but, in addition to this, they
were to 'exercise, by means of sacrifice and sacraments, the work of
salvation which they had proclaimed'. This is a particularly felicitous
account of the mission of the apostles and of their successors. It
distinguishes the two functions of preaching and administering the
sacramental system; and at the same time it indicates how the
second is a development of the first. These two, word and sacrament,
are indissolubly linked in the Church. The liturgy is a form of
preaching Christ to which a new dimension of reality has been given
by God. Because of their sacramental power the apostles not merely
presented a verbal account of the mystery of Christ, an account
which, for all the undoubted power of the Spirit accompanying it
and working through it, remained an objective appeal to the mind
and heart of those who heard it; they could too, in the Mass and the
sacraments, actually bring the faithful into mysterious and efficacious
contact with the Paschal Mystery of Christ itself.

So in Baptism men are 'inserted' sacramentally into Christ's
mystery. The sacrament unites them to Christ in such a way that

his death, burial and resurrection are theirs. Being constituted members of Christ by baptism, they are thereby drawn into that mystical union with him which, according to the divine design, associates them with his supreme work of satisfaction and merit. This association affects them personally so that they undergo an inward, moral rebirth. The life of sin which was theirs is put off; and in this sense they die and are buried. The new life of grace is given them through Christ; and in this sense they rise from the grave, re-born as adopted sons of the Father, qualified to join themselves with Christ in his true adoration of the Father (cf Jn. 4:23). Similarly, as St Paul teaches (1 Cor. 11:26), when they take part in 'the Lord's supper', they are associated mysteriously with the unique sacrifice of Christ and draw upon its saving efficacy; and this the faithful will continue to do until a new form of union with Christ is made possible in his Second Coming.

Article Six concludes with an account of how, according to the New Testament, the Church carried out the two-fold function entrusted to the apostles.

Art. 7. From what has been said it begins to emerge that there is a legitimate sense in which the Church may be said to 'complete' or 'perfect' the work of salvation. Very far from detracting from Christ's unique role as Mediator of salvation, the mediatory function of the Church, since it derives from his, and is subordinated to his, is the supreme proof of the efficacy of his mediation. For the Church never acts independently of Christ; he is always present and active in her saving actions, giving them their power. The mode of his presence varies according to the nature of the Church's action. There is the supreme form of his presence in the Eucharist; but he is present also in the person of the celebrant at Mass in such fashion that it is Christ himself who offers through the priest's ministry. He is present in the other sacraments in a less perfect, but no less true, manner; for it is by his power that the sacraments produce their saving effects. In its formulation of this teaching the Council deliberately retains the traditional expressions which are sufficiently broad to permit of varying theological interpretations. Further, and clearly different, forms of the presence of Christ are realized through the Scriptures when they are read in Church ritual, and, finally, in the prayer of the Church. Christ speaks through the Scriptures; he worships with the Church.

In the second paragraph of this article an important principle is introduced. When he is present in her actions Christ always associates the Church with him in the two aspects of his saving activity, namely, the worship of God and the sanctification of men. In this association is preserved the two-fold relation of the Church to Christ. On the one hand she is wholly dependent on his redemption for all her good works and 'calls upon him as her Lord'; on the other hand, and as a consequence of the first, she herself worships the Father through him, co-operating with him as his Spouse.[2]

The teaching of the first articles is summed up in a definition of she liturgy as 'the exercise of the priestly office of Christ in which the sanctification of man is signified by signs perceptible to the tenses, and is effected in a way which corresponds with each of these signs, and in which also full public worship is performed by the mystical body of Jesus Christ, that is, by the head and his members'. Such a definition justifies the immediate conclusion that celebration of the liturgy is the supreme form of sacred action, unequalled in efficacy by any other action of the Church. For no other action can lay claim to derive its value from so close a relation to the action of Christ or to procure such rich fruits. (This is the sense of the words: 'by the same title and to the same degree'.)

Art. 8. Before concluding the exposition of the nature of the liturgy, the Constitution draws attention to its eschatological significance. Whoever takes part in the earthly liturgy thereby shares in anticipatory fashion in the worship of heaven. The theology developed particularly in the Epistle to the Hebrews is recognizable in this view of the liturgy. Because Christ, the risen Head, has already penetrated in his humanity into the heavenly sanctuary, those of his members who join with him in worship of the Father are drawn into participation in the liturgy of the angels and saints. It is the hope of the earthly members that they will join the company of the saints when Christ comes to bestow the full fruits of salvation in glory.

(b) THE IMPORTANCE OF THE LITURGY IN THE LIFE OF THE
    CHURCH (Arts. 9–13)

The importance of the liturgy is already apparent from the account of its nature; but in these five articles the Constitution further outlines the liturgy's relationship with other actions of the Church.

Art. 9. The limitations of the liturgy are first defined. In spite of its perfection it does not constitute the entire activity of the Church;

2. The relation of the faithful to Christ in worship is more fully developed in *Mediator Dei* (cf CTS [Eng.] ed. §§ 96–98), where, in reference to the Mass, an important distinction is made between offering 'through' and 'with'. Cf *Constit.*, ch 2, art 48.

and indeed men cannot participate in the liturgy unless preachers have first proclaimed to them the Word of God; and, in their turn, preachers depend for their authority on the mission they have received from those who hold jurisdiction in the Church. Not only, then, must the Church call unbelievers to faith in Christ and to repentance; she must continue to preach the same message to believers so that they may be disposed to receive the sacraments profitably. She must teach them to observe the commandments and encourage them to perform 'works of charity and piety' and to exercise the apostolate. (The word translated as 'piety' is *pietas*, which has a technical sense in theology. The Constitution appears to use it in the non-technical sense expressed by the English word.)

Art. 10. Nevertheless, the liturgy remains the central activity of the Church; for it is both the summit towards which every other action is directed and the source from which the Church draws her strength. Each aspect is in turn developed in this article. The text calls for no comment, apart from the description of the Eucharist as the 'renewal of the alliance between God and men'. The redemptive act of Calvary is here considered as the consummation of the Old Alliance between God and Israel and as the seal placed on the New Alliance. For in the person of the Word Incarnate, as he offered his sacrifice, were united both the saving initiative of God and the consequent loving response of man. Here is the supreme expression of the New Alliance and it is only by participation in it that men can be saved. Their participation is achieved by their union with the response of Christ in his humanity to his Father; and this means union with Christ in charity. When Mass is offered and Communion received men enter anew into the Alliance of Christ; the effect of this must be that those who have taken part worthily in the celebration will be urged to the exercise of charity.

Art. 11. It is in this context, where both the limitations and the supremacy of the liturgy are stressed, that the question of the participation of the faithful is first introduced. The present article recalls what is required if the liturgy is to achieve its full efficacy. On the part of the faithful are necessary good dispositions, sincerity in performing whatever part of the ritual may be assigned them, and co-operation with grace. On the part of pastors this implies care that the faithful should participate 'consciously, actively and fruitfully'. No definition is given here of the term 'actively', *actuose*.[3]

3. Father C. Howell, s.j., loc. cit., has: 'fully aware of what they are doing, actively engaged in the rite, and enriched by its effects'; but this is a commentary – however justified – rather than a translation. The German translation is more circumspect with: 'bewusst, tätig und mit geistlichem Gewinn'.

Art. 12. Liturgical participation, however, does not exhaust the demands of the Christian life. Private prayer and mortification are also necessary; and indeed these are the indispensable prerequisites and consequences of true liturgical participation.

Art. 13. It follows clearly that approved forms of prayer which are not liturgical are worthy of high commendation. That they should be in harmony with the liturgy and should lead the faithful towards it is apparent from what has been said of the central place held by the liturgy.

II PROMOTION OF THE FAITHFUL'S PARTICIPATION

(a) THE FAITHFUL'S PARTICIPATION (Art. 14)

By way of introduction to regulations concerning the instruction of the clergy, the Constitution makes certain observations on the participation of the faithful. Since it is in view of promoting such participation that all the subsequent rules are formulated, what is said in various articles about participation itself may usefully be considered first.

Already in Art. 7 it has been noted that Christ always associates the Church with his worship of the Father and his sanctification of men. This applies, though in diverse ways, to both clergy and faithful. Art. 14 expresses the urgent desire of the Church, in her function as Mother, that 'all the faithful be led to that full, conscious and active participation in liturgical celebrations which is demanded by the nature of the liturgy itself' and in respect of which the Christian people, the royal priesthood (cf 1 Pet. 2:9; 2:4-5), has both right and duty by reason of baptism. The same article goes on to state that 'this full and active participation by all the people is the primary and indispensable source from which the faithful are to derive the true Christian spirit'. But what is the precise nature of this participation? Or rather, in order to keep the problem at the practical level which the Constitution favours, what exact form should this participation take?

There can be no doubt that the Council considers it desirable that the faithful should take part in the Mass, for example, by the fullest possible participation in the ritual, answering the responses and joining in the singing, and so on. Does Art. 14 mean that only in this way is the nature of the liturgy fulfilled, and that this form of participation is the primary and *indispensable* source of the true Christian spirit? It must be confessed that no explicit answer is given in the text to this urgent problem. An indication of certain reservations to be made is contained in Art. 19 which distinguishes between internal and external active participation and which admits that the fullest mode of active participation is not in every circumstance feasible. Pastors, it is there stated, must make allowance for differences of age, condition (presumably, sickness and health), way of life (whether, for example, a member of a religious congregation or not) and standard of religious culture. It is necessary on general theological grounds to hold that the conciliar Fathers did not intend to place limits to the internal participation (acts of religion, charity) of any person. It is without doubt at the level of external participation in the ritual that the necessity of allowing for greater or less activity is acknowledged.

From this it is clear that the *indispensable* source of the true Christian spirit is not full external participation. It is, in other words, possible to take part in the liturgy authentically without answering all the responses or singing all that could be sung. From this it follows that the nature of the liturgy does not require full external participation as an inseparable property. It appears necessary to make these distinctions lest imprudent use should be made of Art. 14 as though it required full external participation as an absolute condition for any form of participation whatsoever. Such a maximalist interpretation being excluded, it must be readily acknowledged that the mind of the Council very clearly is that every effort should be made to introduce the faithful to the fullest possible external participation. Only when this is procured will the natural sense of the liturgical symbolism have been satisfied.

By way of theological commentary the following may be said. Participation in the liturgy cannot be exclusively internal. The very nature of the action demands that participation be also external. But simple – so-called 'passive' – attendance at Mass or simple reception of the sacraments are already in themselves external participation. Without doubt the pastoral aim of the Church is that such minimal external participation (which derives from possession of the baptismal character) should be developed to the fullest degree possible. The full potentialities of the liturgy as an action of common worship could be realized only if all the faithful participated fully in the ritual; and each of the faithful should make this his aim. But, as Art. 19 indicates, such an ideal is hardly compatible with the vastly differentiated character of the individuals who make up 'the faithful'. It will be for local bishops to decide, taking account of the Council's wishes, in what measure external participation will be helpful to the majority of their people.

(b) INSTRUCTION OF THE CLERGY (Arts. 15–18)

The prescriptions are of a practical nature. The terms used in Art. 16 – curiously enough in the context – have been given a popular, rather than a theological, signification. It should not be thought, for example, that the enumeration of aspects of the liturgy – theological, historical, spiritual, pastoral, juridical – implies that the last four are non-theological. The exact sense of 'theological' here is probably 'dogmatic' or 'systematic'. Nor is it suggested that the object of theology is 'the mystery of Christ and the history of salvation'. It is a question simply of the practical orientation of theology lectures.

(c) ADAPTATION OF THE TEXT AND RITUAL (Arts. 21–40)

Art. 21 clearly defines the limits set to adaptation of the liturgy. It concerns only the text and the ritual; and the rule guiding it is the faithful's power of understanding. The necessary qualification is added: 'in so far as possible'; for the liturgy is in the final analysis a mystery.

Among the general directive norms, noteworthy is the stress laid in Art. 24 on the place of scripture in the liturgy. The scriptures are not simply the material source from which the text of the liturgy is drawn, either directly or indirectly. The liturgy, because it is the activation of the mystery of Christ, is a sacramental celebration of the scriptures. The word of the liturgy is the word of the scriptures; and in the liturgy the scriptures acquire new saving effectiveness because Christ is present and active in a special way in these Church actions. Art. 35 returns to this theme, showing how the homily also, if based on the scriptures and the liturgy, becomes 'a proclamation of God's wonderful works in the history of salvation or in the mystery of Christ ever made present and active within us, especially in the celebration of the liturgy'.

Arts. 26–32 formulate rules for adaptation based on the fact that the liturgy is an action of the whole Church, involving not only ordained ministers but also the body of the faithful. As Art. 26 stresses, though certain functions in the liturgy are reserved to those in sacred orders, the integral action of the liturgy belongs to the whole Church and shares in the nature of the Church. And the

Church, in spite of its being divided into rulers and those ruled, is a unified body, with the parts co-operating harmoniously in view of attaining a single purpose. The Church, both in its structure and in its worship, is a 'sacrament' or visible manifestation of unity; and in liturgical action this unity is further deepened by Christ.

In the very nature of things, the liturgy, no matter how it is externally celebrated, activates in this way the unity of the Church. This is particularly true of the Mass; and it would be a dangerous aberration if the Council's desire for full external participation were to be interpreted as some kind of condemnation of what are popularly known as 'private' Masses. It is a fact that in certain continental religious communities the practice has been introduced of priests attending the conventual Mass and receiving Communion during it, instead of celebrating personally. While respect is owed the individual's conscience, it must be maintained that if such a practice were to become general the nature of the Mass would be gravely misunderstood. This is something, it seems safe to assert, which the ordinary Catholic's common sense makes clear to him; it can also be demonstrated theologically. It is to be hoped that the brief reference to the matter in Art. 27 – 'every Mass has of itself a public and social nature' – will not be overlooked.

The rules deriving from the didactic and pastoral character of the liturgy (Arts. 33–36) serve to emphasize once again that the liturgy is a celebration of the Word of God in which God speaks through Christ and the people respond to his invitation. The prayers of the community and the symbolic actions performed are all meant to speak to the minds and hearts of the participants, and to encourage them to render intelligent and willing service to God. Such a purpose obviously cannot be achieved if the people do not understand what is going on; whence the need for simplicity and brevity in the ritual (Arts. 33–34). It is in this context that the agitated question of Latin is considered; prudently, no universal solution is proposed, a limited faculty of introducing the vernacular being extended to local authorities (Art. 36).

Similar principles are applied to adaptation of liturgical ceremonial to local and racial customs; and a similar limited faculty of modification is granted (Arts. 37–40).

(d) LITURGICAL SIGNIFICANCE OF DIOCESE AND PARISH
    (Arts. 41–42)

The genius of the Constitution for getting to the heart of things and

sketching out in broad strokes the essentials of the liturgy is again
exemplified in this section. The liturgy, as the people see it celebrated,
is scattered, as it were, piecemeal throughout all the churches and
chapels of the world. All the local celebrations are certainly united
invisibly by reason of the union of each priest and each member of
the faithful with Christ. But with the liturgy, as with the Church,
what is invisible is always accompanied by and expressed by a visible
element. So it is with unity. The bishop is its visible centre in each
diocese. Christ is the unique High Priest; the bishop is for his own
flock Christ's representative and is therefore the visible high priest
of his diocese. Though he is not always able to exercise his pastoral
office directly in respect of all his flock, he retains, ideally at least, a
controlling influence on the liturgical life of the diocese. It is he,
normally, who ordains and confirms; and it is he who consecrates
the materials used in several of the sacraments.

The liturgical unity of the diocese would be ideally signified if all
the priests and all the faithful were grouped around the bishop in a
single celebration (Art. 41). Evidently, it is only in the rarest circumstances that such symbolism can be created. Practical requirements
dictate that the smaller groupings of parishes be set up within each
diocese; and then the symbol of liturgical unity is best achieved
when the local parishioners are grouped around their parish priest.
Common parish worship is calculated to encourage the growth of
that community-awareness which should be characteristic of those
who form one body in Christ, united in charity.

The Constitution passes over in silence the obvious difficulty that
the order of priests is not organized exclusively on a diocesan basis.
This means that the Mass, the principal act of the liturgy, and of the
Church, is not necessarily a diocesan or parochial act. It is quite
true that the greater part of the faithful belongs to one or other
diocese and parish and, for this reason, the parish Mass has a particular significance. The Constitution justly lays stress on the
importance of Sunday Mass in this respect; but even here it hardly
appears that the present juridico-sacramental constitution of the
Church, with its provision for religious orders and congregations,
necessarily requires attendance at the parish church. In harmony
with the spirit of the Constitution, the existence of religious orders
should be seen, not as a threat to the unity of the Church, but as a
witness to the rich diversity of Catholicism. Wherever Mass is
celebrated the Church is one in Christ.

(e) PROMOTION OF THE PASTORAL-LITURGICAL MOVEMENT
(Arts. 43–46)

Introducing regulations concerning the establishment of various
commissions, the Constitution significantly describes the liturgical
movement as a sign of the providential dispositions of God for the
present age and as the passing of the Spirit through his Church. The
provisions made by the Council are themselves among the principal
manifestations of this divine intervention.

Chapter Two

The Holy Eucharist

MICHAEL MYERSCOUGH, C.P.

DOCTRINAL AND PASTORAL INTRODUCTION (Arts. 47–49)

Article 47, the first article of chapter two, gives the doctrinal background for all that follows, the institution of the eucharistic sacrifice
and Our Lord's command that it should be perpetuated 'until he
should come again': his wish 'to entrust . . . a memorial of his
death and resurrection' to his Church; 'a sacrament of love, a sign
of unity, a bond of charity, a paschal banquet in which Christ is
eaten, the mind is filled with a grace and a pledge of future glory is
given to us'.

This leads naturally into Art. 48, which begins: 'The Church,
therefore, earnestly desires that Christ's followers, when present at
this mystery of faith, should not be there as strangers or silent
spectators' – echoes of *Mediator Dei* and 1958 Instruction on Sacred
Music and the Liturgy. With fine precision the part the people should
play 'in the sacred action' is here stated afresh – 'they should take
part . . . conscious of what they are doing, with devotion and full
collaboration. They should be instructed by God's word (does this
look forward to the provision for the vernacular in the readings
mentioned in Art. 54?) and be nourished at the table of the Lord's
body'. In Art. 55 it is strongly commended 'that the faithful receive
the Lord's body from the same sacrifice', in other words from hosts
consecrated at the Mass they offer – in fact the article calls this
practice 'a more perfect form of participation in the Mass'. Art. 48

continues that they should learn to offer themselves 'by offering the immaculate victim not only through the hands of the priest, but also with him'; 'through Christ their Mediator, they should be drawn day by day into ever more perfect union with God and with each other, so that finally God may be all in all'.

'For this reason', Art. 49 states, 'the Sacred Council, having in mind those Masses which are celebrated with the assistance of the faithful, especially on Sundays and feasts of obligation, has made the following decisions in order that the sacrifice of the Mass, *even in the ritual forms of its celebration* (italics mine) may become pastorally efficacious to the fullest degree'.

REVISION OF THE MASS RITE (Art. 50)

Now follows in Art. 50 the decision of the Fathers to revise the rite of the Mass, which is to be done 'in such a way that the intrinsic nature and purpose of its several parts, as also the connection between them, may be more clearly manifested, and that devout and active participation by the people may be more easily achieved. For this purpose the rites are to be simplified, due care being taken to preserve their substance'. This will be done in two main ways:

(1) by *discarding* those 'elements which, with the passage of time, came to be duplicated, or were added with but little advantage';

(2) by *restoring* 'other elements which have suffered injury through accidents of history'.

These are 'to be restored to the vigour which they had in the days of the holy Fathers, as may seem useful or necessary'. If one may make bold to say on what lines the post-conciliar Commission will work with regard to the two points above – and it will be left to a post-conciliar Commission to apply these principles in practice – one would instance perhaps the shortening of the Offertory rite with its accumulation of prayers, the omission of preparatory prayers at the foot of the altar, the so-called Last Gospel; and as regards restorations, Art. 53 instances one important change already 'the Community Prayer' or 'Prayer of the Faithful' which is to be restored on Sundays and holidays of obligation especially, and will find its proper place 'after the Gospel with its homily'. 'By this prayer, in which the people are to take part, intercession will be made for Holy Church, for the civil authorities, for those oppressed by various needs, for all mankind and for the salvation of the entire world'. Learned liturgists have employed themselves for some time in the study of the 'Prayer of the Faithful' or 'Community Prayer' – notably Professor Fischer of Trier, not to speak of Father Jungmann, and according to them it would take the form of a litany to be recited by priest and people in alternation after the 'liturgy of the word', i.e. after the residual *Oremus* that now incongruously adorns the beginning of the Offertory. As Art. 53 indicates, it will include the causes and needs of the people present and may, in the opinion of experts, end with some form of *Confiteor*, to replace the one at the foot of the altar. According to Father Jungmann, this is the moment best suited for the confession of sinfulness after having listened to the ideal image of a Christian given us by the words of scripture and the sermon; and before the Sacrifice-Banquet in which we are to participate freed from sins and imperfections by the 'absolution' and our act of contrition *in globo*.

BIBLE READING IN THE LITURGY (Arts. 51–53)

'The treasures of the Bible are to be opened up more lavishly, so that richer fare may be provided for the faithful at the table of God's word. In this way *a more representative portion of the holy scriptures will be read to the people in the course of a prescribed number of years*' (Art. 51) (italics mine). Many had requested a greater variety in the lessons of the Mass in the form of a cycle of three years or more; the Council itself has not determined this but the post-conciliar Commission will be entrusted with the task. Biblical scholars had already drawn up specimen 'cycles' before the advent of the Council, so the spade-work has been done already.

Homily: In the new Codex Rubricarum (1960) a rubric – n. 474 – was inserted in the rubrics of the missal to the effect that 'after the Gospel, especially on Sundays and feasts of precept, a brief homily is to be given to the people according to circumstances'. The Constitution re-enforces this to the extent that 'at the Masses which are celebrated with the assistance of the people on Sundays and holidays of obligation it should not be omitted except for a serious reason'. What is more important, this article tells us clearly what is its purpose and content: 'By means of the homily the mysteries of the faith and the guiding principles of the Christian life are expounded, during the course of the liturgical year, from the sacred text'; and —what is perhaps more important still in this context-'the homily, therefore, is to be highly esteemed as part of the liturgy itself.' Far from being an interruption of the liturgical rite, the homily or sermon forms an integral part of the service of God's word. According to experts, the structure of the fore-Mass or liturgy of the word is such as to require preaching and exposition of the faith – Epistle, Gospel, Sermon. Father McManus, a theological expert at the Council, says this should be the normal and usual development in which the reading of God's word is incomplete without the living message of the teaching Church. We shall have to wait for more precise instructions on the application of this principle, but the fact that this article states that the homily 'is to be highly esteemed as part of the liturgy itself', that the next article (53) conjoins it with the Gospel – when it states that the 'Prayer of the Faithful' is to be restored 'after the Gospel with its homily' (cf also Art. 78 on Matrimony which 'is normally to be celebrated within the Mass, after the reading of the Gospel and the homily, just before the Prayer of the Faithful') – surely means that henceforth there will be no extraneous matter between the Gospel and its explanation. The homily 'is a continuation of the word of God, a part of the heralding (*kerygma*) of the salvation of mankind through the Word become Flesh, not a catechetical instruction, a pep talk or a meditation on a pious subject of the preacher's own choice' (REINHOLD, *Bringing the Mass to the People*, p. 55, Burns and Oates, London, 1960.) A careful reading of Art. 52 indicates that the homily belongs *especially* on Sundays and holidays of obligation, which means that it is at least permitted, if not desirable, at certain weekday Masses at which the people are present, e.g. in Lent. The practice of a brief homily in such circumstances has been tremendously beneficial in many countries, but is growing only slowly in Britain and Ireland.

VERNACULAR IN THE MASS (Art. 54)

The article begins: 'In those Masses which are celebrated with the people, a suitable place may be allotted to their mother-tongue. This is to apply in the first place to the readings and Prayers of the Faithful, but also, as local conditions may warrant, to those items of the liturgy which pertain to the people, according to the principle laid down in Art. 36 of this Constitution'.

Readers are referred to an article in *The Tablet* (11-1-1964) by Archbishop Grimshaw (member of the Council Commission on the Liturgy, President of a sub-commission of the same, and currently Chairman of a body of English-speaking bishops for the vernacular texts that may be used in the Mass) on this still very much disputed question, the use of the mother-tongue. He makes the salient point that 'the bishops of the universal Church have decided that changes must be made, but that these changes are not unlimited'. Art. 36, states: 1: Though existing special exemptions are to remain in force, the use of the Latin language is to be preserved in the Latin rites. 2: But since the use of the mother-tongue is frequently of great advantage to the people in the Mass . . . the limits of its employment may be extended. This will apply in the first place to the readings and directives, and to some of the prayers and chants, according to the regulations on this matter to be laid down separately in subsequent chapters. 3: These norms being observed, it is for the competent ecclesiastical authority, mentioned in Art. 22 §2, to decide whether and to what extent, the vernacular language is to be used; their decrees are to be approved, that is, confirmed, by the Holy See. And whenever it seems to be called for, they are to consult with the bishops of neighbouring territories which have the same language. 4: Translations from the Latin text intended for use in the liturgy must be approved by the competent local authority mentioned above'.

Art. 36 thus gives to 'various kinds of local bishops' conferences' (cf Art. 22, §2) the power to decide, within the limits of the Constitution, how the vernacular should be used, only seeking confirmation of their decisions from the Holy See; and secondly the same bodies have the power to approve the vernacular texts to be used. It will belong to the local bishops' conferences to determine as soon as possible (according to Bishop Jenny, Auxiliary of Cambrai, in an article in *Informations Catholiques Internationales*, 15 Dec. 1963) what texts recited or sung of the Ordinary of the Mass are 'to be translated and used in the living language of the people' in addition to the Epistle and Gospel and the 'Prayer of the Faithful'. For sung Masses it seems obvious that the *Kyrie*, *Gloria*, etc. will be in Latin everywhere until such time as there will be a wedding between approved translations and sufficiently beautiful melodies if and when desired. Indeed it would appear almost impossible to achieve this until the Missal is revised after the Council. Also, Art. 54, after the paragraph on the use of the vernacular at Mass, states: 'Nevertheless steps must be taken to ensure that the faithful are able to say or sing together, also in Latin, those parts of the Ordinary of the Mass which are rightfully theirs'.

Art. 54 concludes with a very telling paragraph: 'If an even more extended use of the mother-tongue within the Mass appears desirable in some parts of the world, the procedure laid down in Art. 40 of this Constitution is to be observed'. In brief, it means, according to Archbishop Grimshaw, that if changes are desired in those parts of the Mass recited or sung by the priest, the local episcopal conferences must present their suggestions to the Holy See for approval – the new formula granting legislative power to the local bishops was not introduced into Art. 40. He says: 'Our present Art. 54 must be read particularly carefully in as far as it concerns the part of the Mass which the priest says or sings'. If, for example, it was desired to have the Collect and Post-Communion in the vernacular then the means provided in Art. 40 would have to be used. For the chants of the Proper of the Mass – Antiphons for the *Introit* etc. – Bishop Jenny thinks it possible that the permission will be given to use an approved translation, but 'the big difficulty here at present consists in employing a form of music which at one and the same time matches up the living language to the dignity of the sacred text'.

Apart from sung Masses, this has added weight when considering dialogue Masses at which hymns or psalms are sung at the beginning, at the Offertory, Communion and the end of Mass, as is done fairly frequently nowadays. One wonders how many people would prefer to recite vernacular texts at this time? Some think it would be a good idea to use an existing translation (if approved) against the time – 5 to 7 years hence – when the Missal will have been revised. To summarize the provisions of Art. 54 regarding the introduction of the vernacular:

(1) For those parts recited or sung by the people, in addition to the readings and the 'Prayer of the Faithful' (*oratio communis*), the decision rests with the local bishops' conferences.

(2) For those parts recited or sung by the priest – cf Art. 40 – those wishing to introduce changes here must present their suggestions to the Holy See for approval, e.g. Collect and Post-Communion.

COMMUNION UNDER BOTH KINDS (Art. 55)

After confirming 'the dogmatic principles about communion of the faithful which were laid down by the Council of Trent' (communion 'under one kind alone') the article goes on to enumerate the occasions on which 'communion under both species may be granted when the bishops think fit, not only to clerics and religious, but also to the laity, in certain cases to be determined by the Apostolic See – as for instance, to the newly-ordained in their Mass of Ordination, to the

newly-professed in their Mass of religious profession, and to the
newly-baptized in the Mass which follows their baptism'.

The restoration of the chalice to the laity in these special circumstances will be most welcome to all who have the true reform of the
liturgy at heart but it will take some time to bring it into orderly
practice, whereas it is relatively easy to introduce the faithful to
receiving Holy Communion with hosts consecrated at the same
sacrifice – 'a more perfect form of participation in the Mass' the
Constitution calls it.

ONE SINGLE ACT OF WORSHIP (Art. 56)

'The two parts which, in a certain sense, go to make up the Mass,
namely the liturgy of the word and the eucharistic liturgy, are so
closely connected with each other that they form but one single act
of worship'. Pastors of souls are therefore strongly urged to instruct
their people 'to take their part in the entire Mass, especially on
Sundays and holidays of obligation'. One fervently hopes that more
and more people will come to realise the truth proclaimed here –
'the intimate link between the Word and the Sacrament' – concerning which there has been much study among liturgiologists in recent
years. (Cf French Liturgical Week, Strasbourg, in 1957.) 'These
studies show greater affinity between the two parts of the Mass than
was suspected by the preceding generations of pure historians. It
would be a mistake nowadays to attach importance to the "historical
accident theory" by which a fusion took place of the synagogal
service (reading and praying) with the new mystery of the Breaking
of the Bread'. (REINHOLD, op. cit., p. 51.) Father Reinhold sum-
marizes the truth when he says: 'as Jesus was physically present at
the Last Supper, so he is present in his Word during the Fore-Mass'.
(ibid.)

A true appreciation of this point by priests themselves should
lead to a favourable response by their people. One hopes, now that
the homily is to be restored to its rightful place, followed by the Prayer
of the Faithful, that notices and announcements will be reduced
to a minimum, and will not descend to the sort of announcements
that could be carried in parish bulletins and magazines.

CONCELEBRATION (Arts. 57–58)

'Concelebration, whereby the unity of the priesthood is appropriately
manifested, has remained in use to this day in the Church both

eastern and western. For this reason it has seemed good to the Council to extend permission for concelebration to the following cases'. (Art. 57 §1.)

The decision of the Council to commend and extend concelebration in well-determined cases is in line with the principle outlined in Art. 27, that 'whenever rites, according to their specific nature, make provision for *communal celebration* involving the presence and active participation of the people, this way of celebrating them is to be preferred – so far as possible – to a celebration that is individual and quasi private. This applies with especial force to the celebration of Mass . . . even though every Mass has of itself a public and social nature'. On this last point, Art. 57 §2 having said that 'it is for the bishop, however, to regulate the discipline of concelebration in the diocese', goes on to add, 'but each priest shall always retain his right to celebrate Mass individually, though not at the same time in the same church as a concelebrated Mass, nor on Maundy Thursday'.

We are familiar with concelebration at Ordination Masses, and when a bishop is consecrated. The permission for it is now extended to Maundy Thursday (both the Chrism Mass and the Evening Mass), to Masses during councils, bishops' conferences and synods, and at the Mass for the blessing of an abbot. The next section of Art. 57, §1 (ii), continues: 'also with permission of the Ordinary to whom it belongs to decide whether concelebration is opportune, and to regulate the way in which it is done:

(a) At conventual Mass, and at the principal Mass in churches when the needs of the faithful do not require that all priests available should celebrate individually.

(b) At Masses celebrated at any kind of priests' meetings whether the priests be secular clergy or religious'.

We shall all need to do much re-thinking of our ideas before the idea of concelebration and its practice take deep root. Our starting point and indeed 'the point of no return' will be the Council's own words that by concelebration 'the unity of the priesthood is appropriately manifested'. Most priests will be grateful for the extension of permissions: may we live to see concelebration in practice! It would seem still to be a thing of the future, for as Art. 58 decrees – 'a new rite for concelebration is to be drawn up and inserted into the Pontifical and into the Roman Missal'.

Chapter Three

Sacraments and Sacramentals

LIAM WALSH, O.P.

In the language of the Church a 'constitution' is a document that is at once doctrinal and disciplinary: it teaches dogmatic truth and lays down related rules of action. The schema on the liturgy was drafted by the preparatory commission as a constitution. It was proposed that the practical programme of reform should be shown to follow from the very nature and purpose of the liturgy. The Fathers of the Council approved this style and method, and it remains in the text which they eventually ratified. The chapter on the sacraments and sacramentals is a good example of it. The relevant doctrinal principles are set down in n. 59–61. A transition from the theoretical to the practical occurs in n. 62, and the disciplinary principles of reform follow, n. 63–82.

DOCTRINE

The title of the chapter is interesting: 'Of the *other* sacraments and the sacramentals'. The previous chapter has dealt with 'The mystery of the Holy Eucharist', that is to say, with the Mass. The Mass is the centre of the sacramental system: it is itself a sacrament, and it holds all the other sacraments together in a balanced unity. So, once it has dealt with the Mass, including Communion, the Council proceeds to discuss the remainder of the sacramental system, namely, 'the other sacraments and the sacramentals'. This stress on the comprehensive unity of the sacramental order, with the Mass as its centre, is characteristic of the Constitution. Trent had to break down the sacramental system into its component parts; it had to define the number of sacraments, and to analyse the specific nature of each; it had to set forth clearly the special position of the Mass as a sacrifice. Vatican II is able to return to a more synthetic view of the liturgy.[1]

1. Father F. Antonelli, o.f.m., secretary of the conciliar commission on the liturgy, notes the complementary character of Trent and Vatican II in an article in *L'Osservatore Romano* (8 Dec., 1963).

PURPOSE OF THE SACRAMENTS (Art. 59)

The text begins by expressing the purpose of the sacraments in three phases: 'to sanctify men, to build up the body of Christ and finally to give worship to God'. The first phase, the sanctification of men, we can understand readily enough. We learned in our catechism that the sacraments are sources, causes of sanctifying grace. But perhaps our catechism did not take us much farther. Perhaps we were left with the impression that the sacraments were private sources of supply, personal preserves, to which 'I had recourse' for the good of *my* soul. The Council is not satisfied with this sacramental individualism. The sacraments, it goes on, 'build up the body of Christ'. It is in the Church, with the Church and by the Church that I am sanctified. It is the Church which offers me the sacraments and by them she draws me into her social life as the body of Christ. And this membership of the Church leads to the third phase in the purpose of the sacraments, 'to give worship to God'. We are sanctified for worship. All creation is directed to the glory of God. Free, responsible creatures have to be specially directed. They must be sanctified, set apart by grace for God, if they are to promote his glory. And because men are social creatures they are sanctified in a community, for community worship. They become 'a kingly priesthood and a holy nation' (Exod. 19:6). It is this third phase which gives a properly liturgical dimension to the sacramental system.

It is not an unjust criticism to say that post-tridentine sacramental instruction has hardly done justice to the worship value of the sacraments. It expounded admirably their sanctifying efficacy, that downward movement by which grace comes from God to the soul, through the intrinsic power of a validly celebrated sacrament. But it tended to see the upward movement of worship only in the sacrificial aspect of the Mass. Perhaps part of the difficulty came from a rather legalistic habit of reducing the sacraments to their essential 'matter and form', and from a preoccupation with the validity of a celebration rather than with its integrity. There is more to the sacraments than valid matter and form. The Church has designed a full ritual setting around the essential centre-piece, in which there is a constant elevation of the mind to God in praise, thanksgiving, petition, self-oblation – all the upsurge of Christian worship in spirit and in truth. The sacraments are acts of worship because they are each related to the Mass; and through the Mass they share in the paschal mystery of Christ. Even the laws of their celebration show them gravitating towards the Mass. Baptism and Confirmation are stages in a rite of

Christian initiation that reaches its climax in the Eucharist. Penance restores one to eucharistic communion. Anointing of the sick is, when possible, completed by Communion or Viaticum. Orders and Matrimony take place, ideally, within Mass itself. As well as that, Baptism, Confirmation and Orders produce a sacramental character, which is a consecration of men, in varying degrees, for the c lebration of eucharistic worship.

SIGNS (ibid.)

The opening sentence of the chapter continues, 'because they are signs they also instruct'. The sacraments are signs: this is a key principle for understanding their nature and purpose.[2] It is as signs that they achieve their triple purpose already mentioned by the Council: they signify the special sanctifying grace which they cause; they are social signs which build up and manifest the unity of the body of Christ; they are external signs such as are required by the very nature of human worship. The Council takes all this for granted in its phrasing and punctuation of this opening sentence. What it is more concerned to stress is that because the sacraments are signs they must *instruct*. A sign is an aid to knowledge, it helps the mind to identify things and to communicate with other minds. And because the sacraments are signs of supernatural realities they speak, not just for our reason, but for our faith. The Council puts it this way: 'They not only presuppose faith, but by words and objects they also nourish, strengthen and express it; that is why they are called "sacraments of faith".' There are two aspects of the activity of faith mentioned here. We understand the first readily enough: the sacraments presuppose the faith of the Church, and of the person for whom they are celebrated. But the second aspect is, perhaps, less familiar to us: the sacraments cause and express faith. The words of the ritual (scriptural texts and prayers) and the material elements employed *mean* something. That is precisely why Christ chose them and why the Church developed them. Our faith reads that meaning and, 'in the very act of celebrating' it is instructed and comes alive. The Council of Trent insisted strongly that the faithful were to be instructed in the meaning of the ritual of Mass and the Sacraments, so that they could enter more fully into the celebration. In spite of that it would seem that subsequently more attention was paid to the causality of the sacraments than to their value as instruc-

2. It is the first thing established by St Thomas in his treatment of the sacraments, III, q. 60. The idea of sign has already been introduced by the Council in n. 33.

tive signs. More stress was put on the intrinsic power of the rite, especially of its essential matter and form, to cause grace *ex opere operato* than on its value as an exercise of personal faith. The sacraments tended to be seen as *things* which did something, rather than as instruments of an immediate encounter between God and ourselves, in which we were sanctified and God was worshipped. True we have always been instructed to dispose ourselves properly for the sacraments, to prepare ourselves by faith, charity and a right intention. But perhaps we regarded that preparation as somewhat extrinsic to the sacrament itself, something to be done beforehand rather than throughout, and by means of the entire ritual of the sacrament. Take the hypothetical example of a priest who would spend a quarter of an hour in fervent preparation for Mass and then 'fly' uncomprehendingly through the Mass itself, satisfied that his rubrics were correct and that his consecration was valid. Such a celebration would, indeed, give worship to God and make grace available to men. But in so far as it was a routine ritual rather than a living dialogue of faith it would do little or nothing to enlighten and form those dispositions on which the fruitfulness of the sacrament depends. It is this power of 'the very act of celebrating' to cause dispositions of faith, worship and love that the Council wants to stress: 'They have indeed the power to impart grace, but, in addition, the very act of celebrating them effectively disposes the faithful to receive this grace fruitfully, to worship God duly and to love each other mutually'.

The practical conclusion which is drawn from the doctrine of the first paragraph is an exact statement of the programme of what is nowadays called Pastoral Liturgy: 'Firstly, it is therefore of the highest importance that the faithful should easily understand the sacramental signs'. They will understand the sacraments easily if they have that 'noble simplicity' which the Council desires to see in the restored liturgy (n. 34); if they are properly carried out by the minister (n. 18); and if they are explained – although they 'normally should not require much explanation' (n. 34). If the faithful understand the sacraments they will be more likely to carry out the second part of the programme, which is that they 'should frequent with great eagerness those sacraments which were instituted to nourish the Christian life'. They will frequent the sacraments, not simply out of a sense of obligation or because of social pressures but willingly and joyfully.

SACRAMENTALS (Arts. 60–61)

Christ instituted sacraments, to which he gave an intrinsic power of signifying and producing special effects, in his name. The Church cannot, of course, institute new sacraments. But she can do something analogous. In her own name she chooses certain symbolical objects or actions, which she blesses or consecrates with prayer. She offers these 'sacramentals' to the faithful as signs of special graces which they can receive through the intercession of the Church. By the sacramentals 'various occasions in daily life are rendered holy'. But more than that – and this is something we do not always advert to in our devotions – 'by their aid men are disposed to receive the chief fruits of the sacraments'. This gets us back again to the cardinal principle of the unity of the sacramental system. Although the sacramentals are infinitely beneath the sacraments as sources of grace they play their humble part in one great dispensation. Many of them are used in the sacraments themselves or are derived from them. But wherever they occur they are part of the liturgy. They help to maintain, all through life, that contact with the sacred which reaches its periodic climax in the sacraments. As the Council puts it, the faithful 'are given access to the stream of divine grace which flows from the paschal mystery of the passion, death and resurrection of Christ, the fount from which all the sacraments and sacramentals draw their power'. The Council does not enter into the thorny question of *how* the sacramental system makes the paschal mystery of salvation available to us. But it does state the wonderful fact that the mystery of Christ is active in the liturgy, radiating grace into every moment of our lives, sanctifying our actions and consecrating them to worship. Through the sacraments and sacramentals 'there is hardly any proper use of material things which cannot thus be directed towards the sanctification of men and the praise of God'.

DISCIPLINE (Art. 62)

The Council has already explained that the liturgy contains some elements that are unchangeable, because divinely instituted, and others that are human additions that may come and go with the tide of history (n. 21). Liturgical studies over the past half-century have made it possible to distinguish the permanent core of the sacraments from the accessory developments. They have also shown that some of the accessories have tended to obscure the meaning of the sacraments themselves, especially for the people of our own time. The Council candidly makes this criticism its own: 'With the passage of time, however, there have crept into the rites of the sacraments and sacramentals certain features which have rendered their nature and purpose far from clear to the people of today'. And since its stated purpose is to make the sacraments as understandable and accessible as they are meant to be by their very nature 'some changes have become necessary to adapt them to the needs of our own times'. For this reason the Council 'decrees as follows concerning their revision'. The decrees which follow deal with each of the sacraments and with some of the sacramentals. However, they are general principles of reform rather than concrete proposals. The details of reform remain to be worked out by what are being called 'post-conciliar commissions'. In commenting on the text, therefore, we have to remain on a rather general level, with an occasional tentative suggestion by way of illustration.

VERNACULAR RITUAL (Art. 63)

The general principles governing the use of the language of the people in the liturgy have already been laid down (n. 36). They apply without further restriction to the sacraments. One gathers that there was a proposal to insist here that the essential form of the sacraments should remain in Latin. If so it was not accepted by the Council. If the form is to remain in Latin it will be at the discretion of the bishops, not at the command of the Council.

The liturgical book which regulates the administration of the sacraments and sacramentals by priests is the Ritual. The prototype of Latin rituals is the *Rituale Romanum*, published under Paul V in 1614. Although it was not imposed on all the Latin Church, as were other Roman liturgical books, it gradually came into general use. The *Rituale* itself allowed that it could be adapted to local customs and needs, but it was not until about 1930 that advantage came to be taken of this permission on any notable scale. The Holy See began to allow various hierarchies, especially in missionary countries, to use supplements, or appendices to the Roman Ritual. In these the vernacular was introduced in varying degrees, and adaptations were made in the ritual of the sacraments.[3]

What was formerly a concession becomes a command in the Council. Regional ecclesiastical authorities are told to 'prepare without delay local rituals adapted, also as regards the language employed, to local needs'. The Holy See, for its part, promises a new edition of the Roman Ritual. The new local rituals will, on the one hand, be harmonized with this Roman Ritual, and on the other hand adapted to local conditions. Once they have been approved by the Holy See

3. Such a new ritual came into use in Ireland, for instance, in 1961.

they must be 'introduced into the localities for which they have been prepared'. The Council shows once again how preoccupied it is with making the sacraments understood and pastorally effective when it adds: 'In the Roman Ritual each one of the rites is preceded by an instruction, pastoral or rubrical in nature, or referring to the social importance of the rite. These introductions are not to be omitted from the particular rituals or collections of rites which are to be drawn up'. Presumably it wants priests who use the Ritual to have these instructions at their fingertips so that their administration of the sacraments will not just be an exercise in rubrical etiquette, but a meaningful action, both for themselves and for the community of the faithful.

BAPTISM (Arts. 64–70)

In this missionary age adult Baptism is no longer the exception it was during the ages of faith. So the Council re-introduces the catechumenate for adults. At present an adult prepares for Baptism by an intensive course of instruction in catechism. This is not meant to be a kind of cramming, as for an exam. It is part of a religious process, which should prepare the entire person, morally and spiritually as well as intellectually, to adhere to Christ and to enter into the paschal mystery. So it is fitting that the progress of the convert's preparation should be marked by liturgical ceremony, as it was in the early centuries of the Church. 'By this means the time of the catechumenate, which is intended as a period of suitable instruction (*institutio*) may be sanctified by sacred rites to be cele- brated after successive intervals of time'. Presumably the new catechumenate will be inspired by the ancient practice of the *Scrutinia* which were held at various days during Lent in preparation for Easter Baptism. The gradual advance of the catechumen's instruc- tion, and his progressive liberation from the devil, his works and his pomps, will be sanctified by means of prayer and sacramentals, including exorcisms. His sense of reliance on God and the mercy of the Church rather than on his own efforts will be intensified in preparation for the grace of Baptism.

There is obvious scope for adaptation to local custom here. The Council notes that 'In mission territories it is found that some of the peoples already make use of initiation rites'. These are colourful ceremonies which symbolize that, for instance, an infant is received into the tribal community, or young people are promoted from childhood to the adult state. While these rites are, to all appearances,

pagan they may have elements of genuine religious value; and they
always have a powerful psychological and symbolical force for the
people who practise them. Provided they are 'not indissolubly bound
up with superstition and error' (n. 37) they may be admitted to the
ceremonies of Christian initiation.[4]

The ritual of Baptism itself is to be revised. The existing rites,
those for adults and for infants, are of a rather 'makeshift' historical
derivation. The Council wants the different rites reconstructed so
that they will be more realistically adapted to their purpose. That
for adults is to take the restored catechumenate into account; that
for infants is to treat them as infants, and give more prominence to
the roles and duties of godparents and parents; and there should be
variants that would make the baptism of many people together more
practicable. There is also to be a shorter rite 'for use chiefly by
catechists in mission territories, but also by the faithful in general
when there is danger of death, yet neither priest nor deacon is
available'. This will surround the essential matter and form of
baptism, which is all that is said and done nowadays in such an
emergency, with a certain minimum of solemnity and ceremonial.

When an infant who is baptized by the 'short form' survives, the
Church requires that all the ceremonies of Baptism should be
administered in due course. They are valuable sacramentals, and
also help to express the public nature of Baptism. At present the
ceremony is the same as a full Baptism, except that the matter and
form is omitted. Obviously there is a certain artificiality about this:
a child who is already baptized cannot, except by some legal fiction,
be received as if it were still a pagan. So the Council, anxious that
everything in the liturgy should be realistic and meaningful, asks
for a new rite that would 'manifest more fittingly and clearly that
the infant, baptized by the short rite, has already been received into
the Church'. It also wants a new rite 'for converts who have already
been validly baptized; it should indicate that they are now admitted
to communion with the Church', for this is the positive purpose of
the rite.

Finally we must note a significant prescription: 'A special Mass
"For the Conferring of Baptism" is to be inserted into the Roman
Missal'. This is a practical expression of the principle that the Mass
is the key-stone of the sacramental edifice. The meaning of all the
sacraments is clearer when they are celebrated in association with

4. For examples of these rites and of possible adaptations cf *Liturgy and the
Missions*, edited by J. Hofinger, s.j., Burns and Oates, 1960, pp. 209 sq.

it. Baptism is particularly enhanced, because the Christian initiation begun in it finds its fulfilment in the Eucharist.

CONFIRMATION (Art. 71)

There has been a good deal of discussion about the sacrament of Confirmation in recent years. Attempts have been made to relate it to Catholic Action and various other obligations of the adult Catholic life. The age at which it should be administered has been particularly debated. In fact there has been considerable variation in the discipline of the Church over the centuries. Nowadays the Code of Canon Law mentions the 'fittingness' of the present practice which 'delays' the sacrament until the age of seven, but allows that it may be administered to infants in danger of death. Yet it is common practice to delay it until well after the age of seven, and to administer it after First Communion. The Council does not enter into these problems, but it does lay down an important principle about the nature of Confirmation which should appear in the new rite: 'the intimate connection which this sacrament has with the whole process of Christian initiation is to be more clearly set forth'. Initiation into the Christian life is not simply a matter of signing a document; nor is it merely a moral decision to be converted. Ideally it is a progressive sacramental celebration, comprising Baptism, Confirmation and Eucharist, in that order, as well as many associated sacramentals. The present ritual of Confirmation makes the proper effects of the sacrament quite clear, but does not sufficiently show how these effects fit in to the complete process of initiation. The Council mentions the renewal of baptismal vows before Confirmation as a way in which the connection with Baptism could be expressed. It also allows Confirmation to be given within Mass, which would help to show how Confirmation prepares for the Eucharist.

PENANCE (Art. 72)

Here too the Council asks for a revised rite that will 'more clearly express both the nature and effects of the sacrament'. Possibly it is thinking specially of the social nature and effects of Penance. The present ritual is highly individualistic and private. It hardly does justice to the fact that Penance reconciles us to the Church as well as to God, and restores us to full eucharistic communion.

ANOINTING OF THE SICK (Art. 73-75)

It is always difficult to change a well-established name by a peremptory law. The Council wisely allows a gradual transition from 'Extreme Unction' to 'Anointing of the Sick'. It admits both names but states its preference for the latter and, one assumes, hopes it will eventually prevail. There is more to the change than a matter of language. 'Extreme Unction' suggests a sacrament that is administered to people *in extremis*. In our own time people rarely 'send for the priest' until the very last moment, when most human hope is gone. In fact this sacrament is meant for the sick, not just for the dying. (They must of course be seriously ill 'through old age or infirmity' and, to that extent, 'in danger of death'.) The sacrament is meant to give them spiritual strength in their illness and to restore their bodily health. It is so much more effective if the patient is conscious and well enough to take an active part in the ceremony. To increase the realism of the rite, and to allow for various degrees of participation, the Council orders that 'The number of anointings is to be adapted to the occasion and the prayers which accompany the anointings are to be revised so as to correspond with the varying conditions of the sick who receive the sacrament'.

Viaticum is, more properly, the sacrament of the dying, their last eucharistic nourishment on the road to eternity. It may be given apart from Anointing, but for cases when the two sacraments are given together 'a continuous rite is to be prepared in which the sick man is anointed after he has made his confession and before he receives viaticum'. In the present ritual, as a result of various historical accidents, Viaticum is given before Anointing. The revised order is more in keeping with the nature and effects of the two sacraments and expresses once again the culminating place of the Eucharist in the sacramental system.[5]

ORDINATIONS (Art. 76)

The Council wants a revision of the rites and prayers of Ordination. The call for the vernacular will not be so urgent here, as the sacrament principally concerns clerics. But 'The address given by the bishop at the beginning of each ordination or consecration may be in the mother tongue'. This address is a paternal exhortation to those being ordained. It could be less rigid and more touching if spoken in the vernacular. Before ordination to the priesthood there is also an address directed to the clergy and faithful who are present. Perhaps the revised rite will direct itself more often in this way to

5. This order has already been adopted in, for instance, the new German Ritual. It has always been maintained in the Dominican Rite.

the assembled community, which is, after all, deeply interested in those who are being ordained to minister to it. In that case a greater use of the vernacular would be called for.

At present, in the consecration of a bishop, only the consecrating prelate and his two co-consecrators perform the central act, the laying on of hands. In future all the bishops present may do so. This is a return to ancient discipline. Perhaps it is intended as a ritual expression of the collegiality of bishops, and their right to join actively in admitting a new brother-bishop to their ranks.

MARRIAGE (Arts. 77–78)

Not alone must the ritual of marriage be revised, it must be 'enriched' – a kindly thought for this loveliest of sacraments. It is, of course, a spiritual enrichment that the Council is thinking of, 'in such a way that the grace of the sacrament is more clearly signified and the duties of the spouses are impressed upon them'. Since the Council of Trent there has always been a good deal of local liberty about the ritual of marriage. The prescription of Trent on the subject is quoted with approval here. But Vatican II goes even further: 'the competent ecclesiastical authority . . . is free to devise its own rite suited to place and people', subject to the limitations already mentioned about incorporating local practices into the liturgy. But in such new ceremonials there must be no interference with the essential law of marriage, which is 'that the priest assisting at the marriage must ask for and obtain the consent of the contracting parties'.

Marriage, like the other sacraments, is to be closely related to the Mass. It is normally to be celebrated within the Mass, after the reading of the Gospel and the homily just before the 'Prayer of the Faithful'. The Nuptial Mass will include a revised form of the Prayer for the Bride (the prayer said by the priest after the *Pater Noster* of the Mass). At present the wishes and warnings of this prayer are directed mainly to the bride. The revised prayer will bring the groom more into the picture. It may be said in the vernacular and 'will remind both spouses of their equal obligations to remain faithful to each other'. If Marriage has to be celebrated outside Mass the Council orders that at least 'the Epistle and Gospel from the Nuptial Mass are to be read as an introduction to the ceremony, and the spouses should always be given a blessing'. At present the Nuptial Blessing is not given at certain times and circumstances, nor is it ever given outside Mass. In future there will be no such restrictions.

THE SACRAMENTALS (Art. 79)

The prescriptions here are rather general: There is to be 'a revision which takes into account the basic principles for enabling the faithful to participate intelligently, actively and easily'. Such participation will protect the faithful from all shades of superstition in their use of the sacramentals. 'It is lawful even to add new sacramentals as the need for these becomes apparent'. This could be done in mission territories. New Sacramentals might also help to sanctify modern technological civilization as the older ones sanctified rural life. 'Reserved blessings shall be very few . . . in favour only of bishops or ordinaries'. Thus, it seems, priests of certain religious orders will lose the proprietary right they have at present to certain blessings. Some sacramentals may, with due safeguards 'be administered by suitably qualified lay persons'. One might imagine, for example, some sacramentals associated with admission to the lay apostolate being administered by lay leaders.

RELIGIOUS PROFESSION (Art. 80)

Profession is an act of religion that enters closely into the general framework of the liturgy. The Council calls for certain revisions in the rites. The Solemn Consecration of Virgins, a rite proper to some monastic orders of nuns, is to be revised. Presumably it will give clearer expression to the Church's doctrine on virginity, which is an important counterbalance to the teaching on marriage. The ordinary rites of religious profession are at present as varied, and sometimes as fanciful, as the religious habits of monks and nuns. A special rite is to be drawn up, in the interests of 'uniformity (*unitas*), moderation and dignity', which must be used 'by those who make their profession or renovation of vows during Mass'. Religious profession does not have to be made during Mass, but the Council expressly recommends that it should. The religious and sacrificial meaning of profession is powerfully emphasized when, for instance, it is made at the Offertory of the Mass. The common practice of having at least Benediction after the ceremony of profession shows the instinctive eucharistic tendency of profession. Mass would express it even more perfectly, and the unity of the liturgical life around the altar would, once again, be stressed.[6]

6. Cf Rule of St Benedict, c. 58.

BURIAL RITES (Arts. 81–82)

The natural gloom of mourning has tended at times to stifle the joyful hope of resurrection which belonged originally to the funeral rites of the Church. The paschal colour of white, for instance, gave way to sombre black, the *Alleluia* (still found in the eastern rites) to the *Dies Irae*. The Council wants the joy of the resurrection brought back to prominence in the rite. It 'should express more clearly the paschal character of Christian death'.[7] Local traditions and customs are to be taken into account, notably in the matter of liturgical colours. In Africa, for instance, the colour of mourning is not black but red. A new burial rite for infants is to be devised – the present one is simply an adaptation of that used for adults – and a special Mass is to be provided for the occasion.

Chapter Four

The Divine Office

VINCENT RYAN, O.S.B.

Instead of treating successively of all nineteen articles of this chapter, I propose to group the matter in logical order under five general headings: (1) Doctrine; (2) The rhythm of liturgical prayer; (3) The content of the new office; (4) Communal celebration; (5) The vernacular.

DOCTRINE

With regard to the theology of the divine office, Articles 83–87 of this chapter are a faithful echo of *Mediator Dei*.[1] The teaching of Pope Pius XII on the dignity and supreme value of liturgical prayer is here reaffirmed. The pre-eminence of the divine office derives from the fact that it is the prayer of the whole Christ, head and members: 'It is the very prayer which Christ himself, together with his body, addresses to the Father' (Art. 84).

Art. 86 of this chapter disposes of the notion that the divine office

7. See E. H. Schillebeeckx, o.p., 'The Death of a Christian' in *Vatican II: A Struggle of Minds*, Gill and Son, Dublin, 1963.

1. Cf London CTS edition, nn. 146–153.

should be relegated to the background of pastoral life. On the contrary, it is those priests who are most absorbed in pastoral and apostolic work who will have most need of prayer. No amount of missionary activity will bear fruit unless it is sustained by a life of prayer, and no prayer is more efficacious than that spoken by the Church in the sacred liturgy.

The purpose of the new reforms becomes perfectly clear after a careful reading of this chapter. It is not the intention of the Council to curtail liturgical prayer through any lessening of esteem for the divine office, but, rather, to infuse new life into it and to adapt it to the conditions of modern life: 'not less prayer, but better prayer'.

The Council in formulating these decrees was obviously motivated by a deep concern for *truth*, a desire to see the Church's official worship conforming to the norms of authenticity and sincerity. The off-hand manner with which, in the past, we may have satisfied our obligation to the divine office will no longer be considered good enough. There will no longer be any excuse for simply 'getting in' our office at any hour of the day or night, for telescoping the different periods of prayer, nor for the hundred-and-one other anomalies which formerly we took for granted.

The divine office must now become a personal, conscious and deeply interior prayer, in which mind and voice are in perfect harmony (Art. 90). It must become the authentic expression of the personal piety of its minister – priest or religious. In order that this inner harmony be realized, there will be a need for all to acquire a solid biblical culture, and, especially, an understanding of, and relish for, the psalms.

A final characteristic doctrinal feature of this chapter is the manifest importance accorded to communal celebration of the divine office. The superiority of choral, or common, celebration over solitary celebration of the office is based on the fact that the former better manifests the essentially communal character of liturgical prayer. But we must always bear in mind that the divine office, even when celebrated in private, is, of its nature, the prayer of the society of Christians joined to Christ.

THE RHYTHM OF LITURGICAL PRAYER

In response to Christ's exhortation that we pray at all times, the Church has, in the course of the ages, instituted the different liturgical hours. The purpose of these, as Art. 88 points out, is to sanctify the Christian day; and the Council expresses the desire that the traditional sequence of the hours be restored so that they may be truly related to the time of the day when they are prayed. It recognizes, however, the difficulty of putting this principle into practice under modern conditions and the accelerated tempo of living. Our actual method of marking the hours of day and night differs greatly from the old Roman system which divided the night into four vigils and the day into four 'hours', viz., *prima, tertia, sexta,* and *nona;* it is from these that our 'small hours' have derived their names.

A more practical horarium has been drawn up which will enable even the busiest priest to follow the traditional order of hours. Art. 89 lays down the main principles of this reform. First, it declares that Lauds and Vespers being, respectively, the morning and evening prayers of the Church, are to be considered the basic hours of the office, 'the two hinges on which the daily office turns'. This is a return to authentic tradition. Morning and evening will always form the natural divisions of the day. They have always been times specially consecrated to prayer, and from as early as the third century they had a liturgical office assigned to them. Moreover, from earliest times, the hours of Lauds and Vespers had a distinctly public character about them; of their very nature they call for the participation of the faithful. It is for this reason that, further on (Art. 100), the Constitution exhorts parish priests to celebrate these hours in common with the faithful in church on Sundays and on the more solemn feasts.

Compline is the prayer to be said before retiring; hence 'it is to be drawn up so that it will be a suitable prayer for the end of the day'. This seems to mean that the traditional system of three invariable psalms at Compline will be restored; these are psalms 4, 90, and 133, given only for Sunday Compline in the Roman office; considered as night prayers they are admirably chosen for this hour.

The hour of Matins presents a special problem. Liturgically, it is of monastic origin (4th century), but the idea behind it can be traced back to the very ancient practice of prayer at midnight. A very rich symbolism was attached to this hour: it was bound up with the idea of the Parousia, and had the character of a vigil in preparation for Christ's return; for he promised that he would return 'like a thief in the night'. When celebrated in choir Matins will retain its character of nocturnal praise (*nocturna laus*); but it will be so adapted that it may be recited at any hour of the day. Provision is, therefore, made for those who are incapable of observing the traditional hour for this prayer. The adaptation will obviously consist in a new selection of hymns, so that a priest saying his office in the afternoon will not be obliged to intone '*Nox atra rerum contegit* . . .' ('Dark night has covered all the colours of the earth'.)

'The hour of Prime is to be suppressed'. This ruling is by no means arbitrary: the aim is to restore a balance to the morning office, which has become overcrowded. Lauds, as we have seen, is *the* morning office. Prime, on the other hand, a prayer of purely monastic origin, is simply a duplication of Lauds: it is the only hour to disappear.

'In choir the hours of Terce, Sext, and None are to be observed. But outside choir it will be lawful to select any one of these three, according to the time of day'. It is noteworthy that the Council seems to attach more importance to the principle of proper correspondence between the time of the day and its appropriate hour than to the mere volume of liturgical prayer. Certainly, this is a considerable concession to all engaged in the active ministry and will go far to lighten the daily burden of the office. The liturgical hours should now come to be regarded not so much as the *onus diei* (the daily burden) as the *opus dei* (the work of God) which was how St Benedict termed the divine office.

The maternal solicitude of the Church prompts her, in certain circumstances, to authorize total dispensations from the obligation of the office: 'In particular cases, and for adequate reasons, ordinaries can dispense their subjects wholly or in part from the obligation of reciting the divine office, or they can commute the obligation' (Art. 97). The term *ordinary* must be understood according to the definition of canon 198 of the Code of Canon Law: the term includes not only the bishop but, also, the major superiors of exempt clerical religious orders for their subjects.

THE CONTENT OF THE NEW OFFICE

What will the office of the near future be like, and how will it differ from the existing one? The answer to our query is given in broad outline in Arts. 91–93.

The psalms will continue to form the substance of this prayer. But the principle whereby all 150 psalms were recited in the course of a week has not been maintained. Henceforth 'the psalms are no longer to be distributed throughout one week, but through some longer period of time' (Art. 91). What this period will be remains to be seen; some suggest a fortnightly period, as is the custom in the Milanese rite, but it could be extended to a three-weekly or even a monthly cycle.

Matins will be made up of fewer psalms and longer reading (Art. 89). There will be a new version of the psalms: 'The work of revising the psalter, already happily begun, is to be finished as soon as possible . . .'. This announcement may surprise some readers: what of the Latin version of the Psalter published in 1945 by the Pontifical Biblical Institute? It is now recognized that this version, although a scholarly work, is far from satisfactory from a liturgical point of view, being unsuited to choral celebration. The language, although carefully constructed and polished from a classicist's point of view, represents too great a cleavage with traditional Christian Latin: it is the Latin of Cicero rather than that of the great Western Fathers. The psalter of the future will be closer to that of St Jerome, the one with which we are most familiar, but this ancient version will be thoroughly revised in the light of modern scholarship.[2]

The Constitution attaches great importance to the readings of the office. A special place of honour will be given to the reading of sacred scripture, for the Church realizes that the word of God is never so efficacious as when read in a liturgical context. (For a full statement of principle concerning the reading of sacred scripture in the liturgy, cf Ch. 1, Art. 24; also Ch. 2, Art. 51.) There will be longer and better-chosen lessons from the Old and New Testaments.

The same principle with regard to length and variety will hold for the patristic lessons. The repertoire of patristic sermons contained in the Roman Breviary is a rather limited one. Very often the message we manage to extract from a particular lesson has little immediacy or relevance for modern minds. It should be pointed out, however, that to judge these lessons fairly it is necessary to read them in their original context; in other words, it is necessary to read the full sermon as published in the various collections of the Fathers. Originally the full sermon was read in the course of the office; at the end of the medieval period, however, the lessons were drastically shortened with little regard for content or context, with the result that what has survived consists, in many instances, of mere snippets or token readings.[3]

It is to be hoped that the Eastern Fathers will be better represented – one would like, for example, to see included some of the catechetical

2. It is known that Pope John XXIII thought highly of a recent revision of the Latin Psalter executed at the request of the Benedictine General Synod of Abbots: *Psalterii Nova Recensio;* cura et studio R. Weber, m.b. Abbaye S. Maurice et S. Maur, Clervaux, 1961.
3. For an excellent treatment of the lessons of the Breviary, cf *L'Office Divine*, by Dom Pierre Salmon (Editions du Cerf, 1959): ch. IV, *Les lectures de l'office*.

sermons of St Cyril of Jerusalem. The Constitution includes among its 'authors' (*auctores*), 'the fathers, doctors and other ecclesiastical writers'. It seems reasonable to presume that this latter term is wide enough to include some of the great spiritual writers of modern times. (One could, for instance, visualize a sermon by Cardinal Newman being completely at home in such a collection.) The accounts of the lives of the saints will be re-written so as to make them 'accord with the facts of history' (Art. 92).

The hymns of the Breviary are to be revised, or rather restored, Art. 93 decrees: 'To whatever extent may seem desirable, the hymns are to be restored to their original form . . . Also, as occasion may arise, let other selections from the treasury of hymns be incorporated into the divine office'. Here is a long-awaited reform. It was in the seventeenth century by order of Pope Urban VIII that the liturgical hymns were radically revised with a view to making them conform to classical standards of style, expression and metre. The result was a serious impoverishment of these ancient hymns, characterized, above all, by their simple, rugged beauty, and their spontaneous, virile piety. The original versions of the hymns, which have been retained in the monastic office, will now be incorporated into the Roman Breviary.

COMMUNAL CELEBRATION

Art. 95 decrees that 'Communities obliged to choral office are bound to celebrate the office in choir every day in addition to their conventual Mass'. (The communities affected by this law are then listed.)

'Clerics not bound to office in choir, if they are in major orders, are bound to pray the entire office every day, either in common or privately . . .' (Art. 96).

'The occasions on which parts of the office may be replaced by liturgical services are to be defined by the rubrics' (Art. 97). This is an extension of the concession contained in the Code of Rubrics of 1960 (n. 85) with regard to the recitation of the Greater Litanies.[4]

As stated above, the Constitution attaches the greatest importance to the celebration of the office in common. The doctrine of the Mystical Body is the underlying reason for this preference. '. . . Priests who live together, or assemble for any purpose, are urged to pray at least some part of the divine office in common' (Art. 99).

4. Cf 'The Pastoral Significance of the New Code of Rubrics' by Rev. P. Muldoon; published in *Studies in Pastoral Liturgy II* (Ed. V. Ryan, O.S.B.; The Furrow Trust – Gill and Son, Dublin, 1963); cf p. 206.

We may conclude from this insistence on the public character of the divine office that the choral structure of the Breviary, made up of the responsories, antiphons, versicles, etc. will be retained: the Breviary, being the Prayer Book of the Church could never be made to resemble a book of private devotions.

A further stimulus to choral celebration is the rather momentous concession conferred in Art. 96, which particularly affects nuns and others not bound to the divine office: 'Religious who, according to their constitutions, are to recite parts of the divine office, are thereby joining in the public prayer of the Church. The same may be said of those who, in virtue of their constitutions, recite any short office, provided this be drawn up after the pattern of the divine office and has been duly approved'.

This concession will be received with joy and gratitude by great numbers of religious. These short forms of the office which hitherto would have fallen under the definition of *pia exercitia* ('Devotions'), have now been raised to the status of liturgical prayers, with all the prerogatives which that prayer possesses. To understand the difference between liturgical and non-liturgical prayers and actions, the reader would do well to consult the definition given in the 1958 Instruction on *Sacred Music and Liturgy* (Art. 1, Ch. 1). The Instruction states that 'those sacred actions are "liturgical" which from the institution of Jesus Christ or the Church and in their name are carried out in accordance with the liturgical books approved by the Holy See, by persons legitimately deputed . . .'. This mandate to represent the Church officially in its public prayer is now given to all religious. These simple forms of the Breviary will now be included among the Church's liturgical books.[5]

The laity, too, are to be drawn more and more into the Church's official worship: the faithful must also lend their voices to the homage of praise which the Church daily offers to God. Pope Pius XII's desire to see the public celebration of Vespers restored to parish churches as part of the Sunday worship should now be fully realized. Art. 100 lays down: 'Parish priests should see to it that the chief hours, especially Vespers, are celebrated in common in the Church on Sundays and the more solemn feasts'. By 'chief hours' (*horae praecipuae*) is meant the hours of Lauds and Vespers, according to the definition given in Art. 89 (a). As we shall see in our treatment of Art. 101 of this chapter, the use of the vernacular will be permitted at the public celebration of these hours.

5. The best commentary on the article of the Instruction quoted above is that given in *Liturgie et Musique*, by A. G. Martimort et F. Picard. (Editions du Cerf, 1959); cf pp. 21-25.

THE VERNACULAR

As a general principle it can be stated that priests and lesser clerics will continue to pray the office in Latin, whereas almost unrestricted use of the vernacular is granted to religious who are not clerics.

The whole question of the vernacular is dealt with succinctly in Art. 101. It may come as a disappointment to many priests that this latitude with regard to the language of the office has not been extended to them as well. The Constitution, however, makes the following generous provision: 'But in individual cases the ordinary has power to grant the use of the vernacular to those clerics for whom Latin constitutes a grave obstacle to their praying the office as it should be prayed'. The grave obstacle (*grave impedimentum*) could consist in a defective knowledge of Latin or even, perhaps, in a genuine psychological difficulty in praying in that language. Again, it should be noted, as in Art. 97, that the term *ordinary* includes the major superiors of exempt clerical religious orders.

Since the adoption of the vernacular is a great aid towards conscious participation in the liturgy, the Constitution makes the following concession to non-clerics: 'The competent superior (*Superior competens*) has the power to concede the use of the vernacular for the divine office, even in choir, to religious, including men who are not clerics. The version, however, must be one that is approved' (101 §3). It would seem that the term *Superior competens* designates the major superior (and thus, normally, the Provincial), but this is not perfectly clear from the context.

An interesting question arises out of Art. 100 concerning the public celebration of Lauds and Vespers in parish churches. May these major hours be celebrated in the vernacular? The Constitution does not explicitly say so, but this can certainly be inferred from the general principles relative to the vernacular given in the first two chapters of the Constitution (Ch. 1, Arts. 21, 27, 30, 36 §2; Ch. 2, Art. 54). Art. 100 encourages the faithful to pray the divine office with their priests, or among themselves or even individually, and this presumably in the vernacular. Moreover, we learn from the final paragraph of Art. 101 that the priest who prays the office in the vernacular with a group of the faithful, or with religious, is fulfilling his obligation to the divine office.

Chapter Five

The Liturgical Year

VINCENT RYAN, O.S.B.

The chief interest of this chapter lies in its doctrine. It presents us with a splendid theological vision of the liturgical year in which everything is centred on Christ and on his redeeming work. Comparing this chapter with the relevant sections of *Mediator Dei*, we perceive a continuity of thought but also a distinct doctrinal development. By introducing the concepts of the *mystery of Christ* and the *paschal mystery* it completes the teaching of Pope Pius XII and offers a more unified and Christocentric approach to the liturgical year.

THE MYSTERY OF CHRIST

The terms *mystery of Christ* and *paschal mystery* represent key concepts in the Constitution. We are constantly meeting these terms, especially the second of them, not only in this chapter but throughout the entire document, viz., in the introductory chapter (Arts. 2, 5, 6, 10, 16), with reference to the Eucharist (Art. 47), and to the Sacraments and Sacramentals (Arts. 61, 81). The Council has thus brought to fruition the speculation of biblicists and theologians who in recent years have been increasingly pre-occupied with the ideas which underlie these terms.

What is the mystery of Christ? The expression is at first a little bewildering, but a meditative reading of the passages in St Paul where the word occurs will bring its meaning into focus.[1] Basically the mystery is no other than Christ himself considered as the fulfilment of God's eternal plan to save the human race – a plan which is realized in successive stages covering the whole range of human history. The Pauline notion of the mystery of Christ is well summarized by Dom Cyprian Vagaggini in his famous study, *The Theological Dimensions of the Liturgy*[2] in the following passage:

We are therefore remaining faithful to the thinking of St Paul if we use the expression 'mystery of Christ' to refer to everything

1. The most pregnant text is Ephesians 3:1-13; cf also, Rom. 16:25, 1 Cor. 2:7 Eph. 3:9 and 5:32, Col. 1:26.
2. Vol. I published by the Liturgical Press, Collegeville, Minnesota, 1959. Cf p. 9,

that the incarnate Word, Saviour and High Priest of the human race, is and does in the divine plan and its realization. We can equivalate 'history of salvation', 'mystery', 'mystery of Christ': the concern is always with a single reality, in as much as the centre of this sacred history, this mystery, is Christ.

These considerations will enable us to understand the function and scope of the liturgical year so clearly enunciated in Art. 101:

> As each year passes by, she (the Church) unfolds the whole mystery of Christ, from the incarnation and birth until the ascension, the day of Pentecost and the expectation of blessed hope and of the coming of the Lord.

But it was essentially by his paschal mystery that Christ reconciled the world to his Father. In this mystery the passion, death and resurrection of Our Lord form three aspects of a single reality, that of man's redemption.[3] Father Dalmais, in a recent work, has given us this useful and comprehensive definition of the paschal mystery:[4]

> The paschal mystery is the fulfilment of God's great plan for the reconciliation of mankind to himself in Christ and for the summoning of men to share in heavenly benefits by causing to dwell in them the Holy Ghost who initiates them into the divine life.

Immediately we see the importance of the Temporal cycle wholly centred on the saving mysteries of Christ, of which the annual commemoration of the paschal mystery is the summit and crown, and Sunday, the Lord's day, its weekly re-enactment. Easter is not only the heart of the liturgical year, it is also the radiant centre which sheds its light on all the Church's seasons and feasts.

We are now in a better position to appreciate the wisdom of the 1960 Code of Rubrics which had secured the pre-eminence of the temporal cycle. In Arts. 108 and 111 of the Constitution this primacy of the feasts of Our Lord is re-affirmed:

Therefore the proper of the time must be given the preference

---

3. Cf J. A. Jungmann, s.j.: 'The History of Holy Week as the Heart of the Liturgical Year'. Article published in *Studies in Pastoral Liturgy*, vol. I. (Edited by Placid Murray, o.s.b. The Furrow Trust, Maynooth, 1961.)
4. *Introduction to the Liturgy*, published by G. Chapman, London, 1961. Cf p. 78.

which is its due over the feasts of the saints, so that the entire cycle of the mysteries of salvation may be suitably recalled.

PREPARING FOR THE PASCH

To ensure a more fruitful participation of the faithful in the annual celebration of the paschal mystery, the Council has, in Arts. 109 and 110, established the principles for a renewal of the Lenten liturgy:

> The season of Lent has a twofold character; primarily by recalling or preparing for baptism and penance, it disposes the faithful who persevere in hearing the word of God and in prayer, to celebrate the paschal mystery. This twofold character is to be brought into greater prominence both in the liturgy and by instruction.

How will the baptismal character of Lent be brought into greater prominence? One method will be to exploit to better advantage the rich baptismal catechesis contained in the scripture readings. The Lenten Mass formularies have preserved some of the great traditional gospel texts which were once made use of to instruct the catechumens on the mystery of baptism. Unfortunately there has been a displacement. With the disappearance of adult baptism in Rome (6th–7th centuries), these gospels which were originally read on the third, fourth and fifth Sundays of Lent, were relegated to weekdays. The gospels in question are those which are now read on the Friday of the third week of Lent, the Wednesday of the fourth week, and the Friday of the fourth week: they treat of Christ's discourse to the Samaritan woman (John 4:5–42), the healing of the blind man at the pool of Siloe (John 9:1–38) and the raising of Lazarus (John 11:1–45).

These great gospel pericopes which contain a mine of teaching on the mystery of baptism will probably be restored to their appropriate Sundays; in this way greater numbers of the faithful will be enabled to profit by them and so be disposed to renew their baptismal vows on Easter night. The Old Testament readings which accompany these gospels in our missals will also be restored to the Sunday liturgy: in them the sacrament of cleansing and re-birth is admirably prefigured.

We learn from Art. 69 of Ch. 3 (The Sacraments and Sacramentals) that the catechumenate for adults is to be restored, and is to comprise several distinct steps each of which is to be sanctified by sacred rites. It would be very fitting if some at least of these sacred rites were conferred during the Sundays of Lent, thus bringing into greater prominence the baptismal character of this season. This would be a return to the ancient Roman discipline of the catechumenate when, in the course of Lent, the candidates for baptism received the various preparatory rites, known as the 'scrutinies'. The public nature of these ceremonies, each accompanied by a special Mass offered for the Catechumens, was a great incentive for the Christian community to pray for these *electi* whom they would soon be welcoming as brethren and fully-fledged members of the Church.

The penitential features of Lent are also to be given greater prominence, with special emphasis on the social aspect of penance: 'During Lent penance should not only be internal and individual but also external and social'.

The doctrine of the Mystical Body underlies this insistence on the social nature of penance. The Church is not made up of private individuals but of members of a body. Just as the meritorious actions of individual Christians redound to the good of the entire body, so sin inflicts an injury on the entire Church.

There is no question here of restoring the ancient discipline of public penance, but the Church has much to gain by borrowing something of its spirit. The ceremony of the imposition of ashes at the beginning of Lent, for example, is an excellent corporate manifestation of guilt and penance. Other elements in the Lenten liturgy, e.g. the scripture readings, could be exploited to foster among the faithful a deeper awareness of the social consequences of sin. Some public ceremony corresponding to the rite of reconciliation of penitents, which once formed part of the Holy Thursday liturgy, could also be restored.

The Constitution stresses the role of the Church in the reconciliation of penitents: 'the role of the Church in penitential practices (*partes ecclesiae in actione paenitentiali*) is not to be passed over, and the people must be exhorted to pray for sinners'. This is a significant phrase and merits close attention; it should help to counteract the tendency to view the sacrament of penance in too individualistic a light. A citation from Schillebeeckx's *Christ the Sacrament*[5] will form a suitable commentary on this text:

> The ecclesial effect of the sacrament of penance is reconciliation with the Church as the sacrament of our reconciliation with God in Christ. The Church is the earthly manifestation of God's redeeming mercy, and Confession is visible contact with the Church precisely under this aspect. It establishes us in the

5. Published by Sheed and Ward, 1963. Cf p. 217.

ecclesial status of penitents who, by the performance of the penance required by the Church and through the mercy of her absolution, become reconciled with God himself.

THE WEEKLY PASCH

The description of Sunday as 'the weekly Easter' has become a little hackneyed; but while we are familiar with the phrase itself, we are probably far from realizing its full implications. A careful reading of Art. 106 which treats of the Lord's day will leave one in no doubt as to the inestimable importance of Sunday in the mind of the Church. The opening words of this article have the ring of a solemn proclamation:

> By a tradition handed down from the apostles and going back to the very day of Christ's resurrection, the Church celebrates the paschal mystery every eighth day . . . .

The Constitution then goes on to describe in what this weekly celebration of the pasch consists:

> For on this day Christ's faithful should come together into one place so that, by hearing the word of God and taking part in the eucharist, they may call to mind the passion, resurrection and glorification of the Lord Jesus, and may thank God who 'has begotten them again, through the resurrection of Jesus Christ from the dead, unto a living hope' (1 Pet. 1:3).

With that concision so characteristic of the Constitution, we have in this brief paragraph a veritable theology of the Lord's day – a theology of great depth and richness. Sunday is shown to be the day *par excellence* of the Christian assembly, when the faithful gather together in one place to hear the word of God and to offer the Holy Sacrifice.[6] In the sacrifice of the Mass the Church brings to mind the entire saving work of Christ, 'his passion, resurrection and glorification'. In the celebration of the Eucharist the mystery of redemption is sacramentally renewed. To quote again from Vagaggini:

6. Cf Charles Davis: 'The Mass as the Assembly of Christians' in *Studies in Pastoral Liturgy*, vol. II (Edited by V. Ryan, o.s.b. Published by the Furrow Trust – Gill, 1963).

Every Mass expresses synthetically and realizes in its own way
the whole mystery of Christ.[7]

The paschal mystery is then, in a very special way, renewed each
week. That is why the Constitution declares that this day should be
one of joy and of freedom from work. It is in the sacramental
renewal of the paschal mystery that the People of God give thanks to
God 'for his unspeakable gift' (2 Cor. 9:15) – the gift of redemption.

A splendid unity is seen to exist between the two parts of the Mass,
viz., the liturgy of the word and the eucharistic sacrifice. It is in
hearing God's wonderful deeds, the *mirabilia Dei*, proclaimed in the
service of the word, that the faithful are disposed to take their part
in the offering of the Mass itself.

It follows from these considerations that the Lord's day must
enjoy a place of pre-eminence in the Christian calendar. The Council
has conceded to it a dignity that is only surpassed by that of Easter
itself: 'Hence the Lord's day is the original feast day (*primordialis
dies festus*) . . . Other celebrations, unless they be truly of great
importance, must not have precedence over the Sunday which is the
foundation and kernel of the whole liturgical year' (italics my own).

THE SAINTS

The Constitution in assigning to the sanctoral cycle a subordinate
place in the liturgical year, in no way derogates from the cult of the
saints. The liturgical seasons and the feasts of Our Lord must be
given precedence, but, fundamentally, there is no opposition between
the temporal and sanctoral cycles in the Christian calendar.

The Constitution, in stressing the Christological aspect of the
sanctoral cycle, brings to light the underlying unity that exists between the two cycles. The saints by their lives echo the cry of St
Paul, 'I live, now not I, but Christ liveth in me' (Gal. 2:20). In the
saints Christ relives his paschal mystery. We are here reminded of
the theme, so dear to St Cyprian and the early Fathers, of Christ
victorious in his martyrs: 'and he who overcame death for us, ever
overcomes it in us'.[8]

It is not only the martyrs, but the *confessores*, too, who manifest
the paschal mystery in their lives. They share Christ's victory over
sin and death not by laying down their lives but by the perfection

7. Op. cit., p. 75.
8. Epistle X.

of their faith and witness: 'this is the victory that triumphs over the world, our faith' (1 John 5:4).

Sanctity is but the full blossoming of the grace received at baptism by which we are drawn into the mystery of Christ's death and resurrection. Thus, in the opening chapter of the Constitution (Art. 6), we are told that 'by baptism men are plunged into the paschal mystery of Christ; they die with him, are buried with him and rise with him . . .'.

Christian perfection is the realization on the moral plane of the mystery inaugurated at baptism. As Abbot Marmion so well expressed it in *Christ the Life of the Soul*:[9]

> Christian life is nothing else but the progressive and continuous development, the practical application throughout our whole life, of this double supernatural result of 'death' and of 'life' produced by Baptism.

Perhaps these considerations will help us to grasp the force and import of expressions such as: 'By celebrating the passage of these saints from earth to heaven the Church proclaims the paschal mystery achieved in those who have suffered and been glorified with Christ' (Art. 104).

The Constitution thus guards us against an exaggerated cult of the saints and from the tendency to view them as isolated individuals unrelated to the mystery of Christ. In the liturgy the Church contemplates Christ in his saints. The endless variety of sanctity which they display and which is the effect of the multiform grace of God, reflects something of the infinite riches of Christ. This is an added reason for our honouring the saints and is clearly indicated in Art. 111: 'For the feasts of the saints proclaim the wonderful works of Christ in his servants, and display to the faithful fitting examples for their imitation'.

The privileged place which Our Lady has always held in the Church's cycle of feasts is solemnly re-affirmed in Art. 103, but again in the context of the mystery of her divine Son.

> In celebrating this annual cycle of Christ's mysteries, Holy Church honours with special love the Blessed Mary, Mother of God, who is inseparably involved in the saving work of her

---

9. Part 2, section 2 ('Death and Life').

Son. In her the Church holds up and admires the most perfect fruit of the redemption . . .

APPENDIX: REVISION OF CALENDAR

A declaration of the Council on the revision of the Calendar is added as an appendix to Ch. 5. An interesting account of the debate on this subject and that of a fixed Easter is given by Father Antoine Wenger in his book *Vatican II: Première Session*.[10]

Concern was expressed by many of the Fathers at the divorce between the civil and liturgical calendars. 'The Church would like to avoid this hiatus in order to continue, as in ages past, to impregnate the rhythm of time with the Christian spirit which has its source in the paschal cycle'.

It seems that Cardinal Feltin was the leading advocate of this reform. He strongly urged the establishment of a fixed date for the celebration of Easter. The reasons which he adduced were mainly pastoral: such a reform would greatly facilitate the pastoral life of parishes as well as the organization of dioceses. He also remarked that in France, as well as in other countries, school and university holidays were no longer made to coincide with the actual date of Easter. The result of this divergence was a notable depreciation of Easter in civil life as well as a falling off of attendance at the Holy Week ceremonies.

In consideration of these and similar views the Constitution declares that 'The sacred Council would not object if the feast of Easter were assigned to a particular Sunday of the Gregorian Calendar, provided that others whom it may concern, especially the brethren who are not in communion with the Holy See, are agreed on this matter'.

The proviso with regard to the separated brethren introduces a delicate ecumenical note. The Eastern Churches did not follow Rome's example when, under Pope Gregory XIII, it decided on a reform of the Julian Calendar. Today a double calendar is in use in the Greek Churches: the Julian Calendar is followed for the paschal cycle, the Gregorian Calendar for the fixed feasts. In the Russian Church only the Julian Calendar is employed.

Although the fixation of Easter would represent a departure from tradition, the scholars seem to be agreed that there is here no liturgical principle at stake. An authority on the Christian calendar,

10. Published by Editions du Centurion, Paris, 1963 (Series, L'Eglise en son Temps); cf pp. 94 ff.

Mme Noële Denis-Boulet, sees no reason 'why it (the Christian religion) should be tied indefinitely to a luni-solar calendar . . . whose grave imperfections were felt by liturgists long before modern States worried about them'.[11]

As to the actual date to be assigned to Easter, this author suggests the first Sunday after 7 April (the date on which, according to most exegetes, Jesus underwent his passion in the year 30).

Chapter Six

Sacred Music

KIERAN O'GORMAN

Article 113 of the brief but eloquent chapter on Sacred Music states:

> Liturgical worship is given a more noble form when the divine offices are celebrated solemnly in song, with the assistance of sacred ministers and the active participation of the people.

The musical tradition of the Church is very highly valued by the Council which places it above any other art, because it forms 'a necessary or integral part of the solemn liturgy'. This high place has been earned especially by Gregorian Chant which, in a sense grew up with the liturgy and is still to be given pride of place in liturgical functions (Art. 116). But Gregorian Chant is wedded to the Latin language and this is a union which no man should put asunder.

What then will happen now that it is possible that the vernacular may be used in parts of the Mass? (Those who may want to sing the Office in the vernacular will be very few.) This question raises many problems the solution to which can only be guessed at until more directives have come and our hierarchy have decided what parts of the Mass, if any, will be sung in the vernacular. Yet it may not be out of place to examine some of these problems.

The Constitution recommends that in those Masses, which are celebrated with the people, a suitable place may be allotted to their mother-tongue. 'This is to apply in the first place to the readings and Prayer of the Faithful, but also as local conditions may warrant, to

11. *The Christian Calendar;* a Faith and Fact Book (London: Burns and Oates 1960); cf pp. 108 ff.

those items of the liturgy which pertain to the people . . . Nevertheless steps must be taken to ensure that the faithful are able to say or to sing together also in Latin, those parts of the Ordinary of the Mass which are rightfully theirs' (Art. 54). This seems to say that while they may sing pieces in the vernacular (if the bishops permit it or think it wise) the people must also know these chants in Latin. I can see very little need for discarding the Greek phrases *Kyrie eleison, Christe eleison*. These were retained when the Roman Church began to use Latin instead of Greek and are easily learned and understood. Besides, they have the advantage of good musical settings. There are eighteen settings, not counting the 'adlibitum' chants, in the Graduale and though most of these are too elaborate and too outmodish (if I may give the word a slight twist) for good congregational singing, they are but a fraction of some 200 settings. Many of these may be made available in the new editions of liturgical songbooks which are to be completed, or in the edition to be brought out containing simpler chants for use in small churches (Art. 117).

Incidentally, this directive to provide books for smaller churches and the appeal to composers to provide also for the needs of small choirs and for the active participation of the entire assembly of the faithful (Art. 121) shows a very welcome pastoral note missing in previous pronouncements on sacred music.

If a modern setting of the *Kyrie* is to be selected it should be one which is agreed on not only throughout Ireland but also England, Scotland, Wales and if possible America.

The *Gloria* and the Creed are both rather long chants which the ordinary congregation should not be expected to pray-sing in Latin. Indeed many of those now singing them know little beyond the facts that the *Gloria* is a hymn of praise and the *Credo* a profession of faith. But how can they praise when they do not know the words they are using, how can they make an act of faith when they do not know just what it is in which they are professing belief? It would seem desirable that these chants, at least, should be in the mother-tongue. There is some speculation that the Nicean Creed may be replaced by the Apostles' Creed, while in Holland they are urging that in its place we should sing a 'gospel song' based on the gospel of the day.

The same can hardly be said of the *Sanctus*. This is a rather short chant containing but some twenty words easily understood. If the Preface is to remain in Latin and if, as is likely, the celebrant will sing the *Sanctus* with the congregation before beginning the *Te Igitur*, then it would be a pity to break into another language, and perhaps into another melody, when the simple, noble melody of *Sanctus XVIII* flows naturally out of the melody of the Preface.

The *Agnus Dei* is, in a very real sense, out on its own. It does not flow from the action of the Mass but was introduced to occupy the congregation during the 'breaking of the bread' (a rather long ceremony in the early Church). It makes a fine preparation for Holy Communion.

The Choir has two types of chant to sing at a High Mass or *Missa Cantata*. One is the processional chant – Introit, Offertory and Communion; the other is the responsorial – Gradual, Tract and/or Alleluia. This latter type, known as the *canto di riposo* in Italian, was the musical highlight of the Mass and gave its name to the book containing the chants of the Mass, the 'Graduale'. Since then the musical emphasis has shifted to the parts of the Mass belonging to the congregation. Now, that the aim of the restoration of the liturgy is clearly stated to be the active participation by the people, we may expect that the processional chants will be adapted in such a way that the people will join in them by repeating a refrain – in the same way as the 'Gelineau' psalms are sung – and the choir's main function, apart from leading and assisting all the singing, will be to cloak the moment of meditative silence after the reading of the first scripture lesson with an aura of prayer.

Finally, there are the chants of the sacred ministers. If the epistle and gospel are to be chanted in the vernacular, a suitable recitatif must be found. At present, a group of church musicians are working on this problem, trying to find a recitatif which would suit many languages. The difficulty is that each language has its own peculiar cadences and it is at these that the musical inflections are made.

These are some of the speculations to which the Constitution give rise.

A few other points may be worth noting. According to Art. 50 'elements in the Mass which came to be duplicated are to be discarded'. This will mean that the celebrant no longer will have to read the Introit, Gradual, Tract Alleluia, Sequence, Offertory or Communion since these will be sung by the Choir and people, or the *Kyrie, Gloria, Credo, Sanctus* and *Agnus Dei*. Each person will 'do all of, but only, those parts which pertain to his office . . .' (Art. 28). This may lead to a marked difference between what is read at a Low Mass and at a High Mass. The pipe organ is to be given preference in the church, but other instruments may be admitted with the knowledge and consent of the competent territorial authorities.

Stress is again laid on the teaching and practice of music in all religious houses and seminaries. This means there must be competent musical teachers and in this context it is to be hoped that better use will be made in the future of the Pontifical Institute of Sacred Music in Rome.

It is good to read the recommendation that a more critical edition of books of sacred music is to be published. Readers of the *Irish Ecclesiastical Record* who may remember the controversies engaged in by the late Father Bewerunge in 1906 will welcome this. In fact, the critical editions of the Kyriale and Graduale are almost ready.

It is likely that as new church music will be needed, composers will be encouraged to turn their minds to other pieces rather than those of the Common of the Mass. They should be protected by the laws of copyright and the large-scale copying which now exists should be discouraged.

There will be large-scale changes which may take many decades before they are finalized. The aim remains as that stated by St Pius X sixty years ago, that the people must take an active part in the liturgy. We cannot boast that we have listened in the past. When the competent ecclesiastical authorities set up a liturgical commission to regulate pastoral liturgical action throughout the territory, let each resolve to co-operate as best he can so that full use may be made of the liturgy as 'the outstanding means whereby the faithful may express in their lives and manifest to others, the mystery of Christ and the real nature of the true Church' (Art. 2).

Chapter Seven

Sacred Art

DONAL O'SULLIVAN, S.J.

Chapter seven of the Constitution on the Sacred Liturgy, *Of Sacred Arts and Furnishings*, must be read in the light of the preceding chapters. These chapters make repeated references to the Paschal Mystery and to the insertion of the Christian into it by his participation in the liturgy. It is a re-formed liturgy; and this final chapter of the Constitution indicates that a re-formed art is to go hand in hand, or rather, soul in soul with it. In this respect Art. 107 of Ch. 5 would seem to be of capital importance. 'The liturgical year is to be revised so that the traditional customs and training methods of the sacred seasons shall be preserved, or else restored to suit the condition of modern times; their specific character is to be retained, so that they duly nourish the piety of the faithful who celebrate the mysteries of Christian redemption, especially the paschal mystery'. The same emphasis, though this time from a more legal aspect, is perceptible in Art. 128. It deals with laws on art, architecture and furnishings. 'Any laws which seem less suited to the reformed liturgy are to be brought into harmony with it, or else abrogated'.

The opening sentences of this chapter on the arts pleads, like Gerard Manley Hopkins, that beauty be given back to God, 'beauty's self and beauty's giver'. 'All things set apart for use in divine worship should be truly worthy, becoming and beautiful'. The Church reserves to herself the right to judge what is 'fitted for sacred use'. But she 'has admitted changes in materials, style or ornamentation prompted by the progress of the technical arts with the passage of time'.

Art. 123 should settle the perhaps over-acrimonious disputes of recent years as to the existence of an ecclesiastical 'style'. 'The Church has not adopted any particular style of art as her very own: she has admitted styles from every period according to the natural dispositions and circumstances of her peoples, and the needs of the various rites. Thus, in the course of the centuries, she has amassed a treasury of art which must be very carefully preserved. The art of our own days, coming from every race and region, is also to be given free scope provided that it adorns the sacred buildings and holy rites with due reverence and honour; thereby it is enabled to contribute its own voice to that wonderful chorus of praise in honour of the Catholic faith sung by great men in times gone by'.

After the Council, then, there can be no question as to the right of contemporary art to praise God and edify his children, provided it brings 'due reverence and honour' to its elevated task. 'Noble beauty' not 'sumptuous display' is laid down as the norm for bishops in their choice of 'a truly sacred art'. They are 'carefully and insistently' to remove works 'which do not accord with faith, morals and Christian piety and which offend true religious sense either by depraved forms or by lack of artistic worth, mediocrity and pretence' (Art. 124). The Council has previously described in the Constitution the ideal of Christian piety – it differs from the popular acceptation of the word – and one of its main tasks has been precisely to recall us to a *true* religious sense as opposed to an empty and false traditionalism. Following Pope John, it is substituting genuine tradition for fossilized conventions. Many of the laity, many priests too, have become attached to these conventions; and one must not underestimate the imaginative shock they are bound to experience when the 'depraved forms' of the commercialized Hollywood-type 'art' are taken from them. 'Lack of artistic worth, mediocrity and pretence' is only too terribly descriptive of the content of many churches. Bishops are indeed worthy of sympathy, not criticism, in the herculean task which has been imposed upon them by this one paragraph of the Constitution.

Not that the Council has fallen, after the lapse of centuries, into a new iconoclastic heresy! 'The practice of placing statues and pictures in churches so that they may be venerated by the faithful is to be maintained; but their number should be moderate and their relative positions should exemplify right order'. And why the importance of this right order? 'For otherwise they might corrupt the people's sense of values and foster devotions of doubtful orthodoxy' (Art. 125). It is that 'sense of values, that Pope John and his Council have restored to the *plebs sancta Dei*.

And what of the Church's churches? A wise brevity is here the soul of her architectural brief. 'And when churches are to be built, ordinaries must see to it that the design of these churches is such as to facilitate the celebration of the liturgy and the active participation of the faithful'. Cologne and Canterbury – for all their beauty – are not the Council's models for today.

Are, then, bishops whose days are so crowded with grave administrative problems, and who have quite feasibly and unblamedly little aesthetic training, to become architects and artists and men of sure taste overnight? The Council has no illusions on this point. Its instructions are clear. 'When passing judgment on works of art, local ordinaries must listen to the opinions of the Diocesan Commission of Sacred Art and – in those instances which call for it – also to those of others who are specially expert' (Art. 126).

Amongst the 'specially expert' may we not legitimately hope to find those whose lives are dedicated to art? 'Bishops should have a special concern for artists, so as to imbue them with the spirit of sacred art and of the sacred liturgy'. And the Council envisages the foundation of 'schools or academies of sacred art . . . so that artists and craftsmen may be trained' (Art. 127). So, eight hundred years ago, did Gothic grow from all the varying French regional styles when Suger called artists and craftsmen to the Ile-de-France 'from all parts of the kingdom'.

That it is genuinely 'creative' art the Council has in mind and not a soulless St Sulpicerie is shown in its advice to the artist. 'All artists who, prompted by their talents, desire to promote God's glory in the Church, should ever bear in mind that they are engaged in a kind of holy imitation of God the Creator, and are concerned with works destined to be used in Catholic worship, to edify the faithful and to foster their piety and their religious formation' (Art. 127). *Gloriae Dei in Ecclesia sancta servire*! Had the Fathers of the Council wished to devise a motto for the sacred art schools they envisage they could hardly have found one more succinct and more meaningful.

The future of church art, just as the future of the Church herself, depends to a great extent on the good will and the enlightenment of her priests. So 'clerics are to be taught about the history and development of sacred art, and about the basic principles governing the production of its works' (Art. 129). It is the co-operation of priests so trained with the creativeness of the genuine artist that will ensure the fulfilment of the Council's wishes that 'all things set apart for use in divine worship should be truly worthy, becoming and beautiful, signs and symbols of the supernatural world' (Art. 122).

The New Formula for Holy Communion

The Latin text of the decree on the formula to be used in the distribution of Holy Communion is as follows:

Quo magis actuose et fructuose fideles Missae sacrificio participent, et in ipso communionis actu fidem in sacrosanctum Eucharistiae mysterium profiteantur, quam plures preces Beatissimo Patri Paulo PP. VI adhibitae sunt, ut aptiore formula Corpus Domini nostri Jesu Christi fidelibus distribuatur.

Sanctitas porro Sua haec vota benigne suscipiens statuere dignata est ut in sacrae communionis distributione, seposita praesenti formula, sacerdos dicat tantum: 'Corpus Christi', et fideles respondeant: 'Amen', et inde communicentur. Quod quidem servandum erit quoties sacra communio distribuitur tam in Missa quam extra Missam.

Contrariis quibuslibet, etiam speciali mentione dignis, minime obstantibus.

Ex Secretaria Sacrae Rituum Congregationis, die 25 april, 1964.

ARCADIUS M. Card. Larraona
Praefectus.
+ Henricus Dante
Archiep. Carpasien.
a Secretis.

The following is our own translation of the decree:

Many requests have reached His Holiness, Pope Paul VI, for the introduction of a more suitable formula to accompany the distribution of the Body of Our Lord Jesus Christ to the faithful; this to the end that the faithful might participate more actively, and with greater fruit, in the sacrifice of the Mass, and might profess their faith in the sacred Mystery of the Eucharist in the very act of communion.

His Holiness, therefore, acceding to this request, has been pleased to decree that the present formula used in the distribution of Holy Communion be abandoned, that the priest say only: 'Corpus Christi', the faithful replying: 'Amen', and then receiving Holy Communion. This is to be observed whenever Holy Communion is distributed, both inside and outside of Mass; and this no matter what stands to the contrary, even if it be worthy of special mention.

From the Secretariate of the Sacred Congregation of Rites, 25 April, 1964 (cf. *AAS*, LVI, pp. 337-338).

HISTORY

The following short account of the history of the phrase, *Corpus Christi*, is taken from Father Josef Jungmann's *The Mass of the Roman Rite*, vol. 2, pp. 388-389 (Benzinger, New York, 1955). The footnotes, however, are omitted and the Latin and Greek phrases are put into English:

The distribution of the sacrament was accompanied with corresponding words even in the early Christian era. The ordinary form of distribution was: 'The Body of Christ'. This had the significance of a profession (of faith), as the Arabic *Testamentum Domini* explicitly indicates when it describes the formula: 'as the priest gives the Eucharistic Bread to each one, let him testify that it is the Body of Christ'. The same was repeated with the chalice, where, however, the formula was often expanded: 'The Blood of Christ, the cup which saves'. Also, when giving the species of bread, expanded formulas were in use at an early period. Such expanded versions are also seen in the later oriental liturgies. Reverential epithets were added, as in the Greek liturgy of St Mark: 'The holy Body of our Lord, God and

Saviour, Jesus Christ'. Besides this, where possible, the recipient was even mentioned by name, and when the occasion demanded, with his ecclesiastical title, as in the Byzantine Mass, where, as also with the Syrians, the wish was added: 'For the forgiveness of his sins and unto eternal life'. Or the profession character of the formula was underlined, as with the Coptic: 'This is in truth the Body and Blood of Emmanuel, our Lord', whereupon the communicant answered: 'Amen. I believe'.

In the liturgy of the city of Rome in the early Middle Ages, the old tradition of handing out the sacramental species with a corresponding phrase seems to have been broken. . . . What later appears among the Franks is not the ancient profession: 'The Body of Christ', which demands the actualizing *Amen* of the communicant, but instead is a blessing, which is said, in general, by the priest.

THE SPIRIT BEHIND THE ANCIENT PRACTICE

The decree indicates that the restored observance is a profession of faith and that, of itself, it is calculated to make the faithful's participation in the Eucharist sacrifice-sacrament more active and more fruitful. In this context it should be especially obvious that 'active participation' must not be taken to refer to a merely external activity. What is envisaged is personal involvement in an external rite: the joining together of heart and lips in an act of faith such as people elicit with the words: 'My Lord and my God'.

That such an act of faith at the moment of communion will make the communicant's Mass and Communion more fruitful is, in one sense, but an application of the general theological principle that acts of virtue are meritorious (see St Thomas, *Summa Theologiae*, II-II, q. 2, a. 9). But there is, perhaps, yet another sense in which the communicant's *Amen* at the moment of communion can make it more fruitful. At the very centre of Holy Communion is an act of love, or, rather, two acts of love, God's love and the communicant's. One notes, in this connection, the felicitous phrase employed by the decree itself: 'in the very act of communion, *in ipso communionis actu*'. This act of union (or comm-union) is encompassed by love, and an explicit act of faith at this moment focuses a communicant's supernatural love and intensifies it. And it is supernatural love, principally, which enables a man to merit (I-II, q. 114, a. 4).

It might also be suggested that the new observance is calculated to benefit our faith. Muscles become flabby if they are not exercised, and somehing analogous happens to little-used virtues (I-II, q. 53, a. 3). The Eucharist is rightly called the 'sacrament of faith', and it presents the faithful with a recurring and immensely valuable opportunity of exercising their faith in the central mystery of Christ, in the very presence of the mystery. It is difficult to overestimate the value of this new observance, at the time of such crisis and danger for the Christian faith.

BELIEF IN THE EUCHARIST

Of the acclamations which form part of the faithful's response in liturgical celebrations, 'the most important, if one is to judge by the frequency
with which it is described and commented by the Fathers, is the *Amen*,
which has passed untranslated from the Jewish liturgy into the New
Testament and into the Christian liturgy. In the early centuries, it was
characteristic of the active participation of the faithful at Mass, it was a
profession of faith in the Eucharist, it ratified prayers and wishes' (*L'Église
en Prière*, ed. A. Martimort, Paris, 1961, p. 131). The word *Amen* comes
from the same Hebrew root as the verb 'to believe' (see entry in *Vocabulaire
de Théologie Biblique*) and it is this meaning which is uppermost in its
use in the restored formula.

The following two quotations from the Fathers (in our own translation)
show how they saw the use of the *Amen* in the Eucharistic context. The
first is from St Ambrose, *De Sacramentis*, 5:25:

> When you say *Amen*, it is not an empty gesture: you have already
> said in spirit that you would receive the Body of Christ. When,
> therefore, you present yourself to the priest, he says to you: 'the
> Body of Christ' and you answer *Amen*, which means, 'That is so'.
> What your tongue says, you should accept in your heart.

The other passage is from St Augustine, Sermon 272 (PL 38, col. 1274).
It is particularly valuable for a fuller understanding of our Eucharistic
faith:

> If you would understand what the Body of Christ is, listen to what
> the Apostle tells the faithful: 'For you are the Body of Christ, and
> his members' (1 Cor. 12:27). If therefore you are the Body of Christ
> and his members, it is your mystery which is placed on the Lord's
> table. It is your mystery which you receive. When you reply, *Amen*,
> you are saying *Amen* to what you yourselves are. What you hear is
> 'The Body of Christ', and what you reply is *Amen*. Be therefore, in
> fact, each of you a member of Christ, so that your *Amen* will ring true.
>
> But why bread? In this matter we shall offer no theory of our own;
> let us hear the same apostle who, speaking of the Sacrament, said:
> 'For we, being many, are one bread, one body' (1 Cor. 10:17).
> Understand this and be glad; unity, truth, piety, charity. 'One bread'
> —what does this mean? 'being many, are one body'? Remember
> that you cannot make bread from one grain of wheat, you need many.
>
> When you were exorcised, it was as though you were being put
> through the mill. When you were baptized, it was as though you were
> being moistened. When you received the fire of the Holy Spirit, it
> was as though you were put in the oven. Be therefore what you per-
> ceive, and receive what you yourselves are. . . .
>
> It was by these that Christ the Lord symbolised us and wished to
> bind us to himself. He consecrated the mystery of peace and our
> unity on his table. If a man receives the sacrament of unity, and does
> not keep the peace, the sacrament will not benefit him, but will stand
> in evidence against him.

The Constitution
on the
Sacred Liturgy

CONTENTS

INTRODUCTION

1°. The Sacred Council has for its objectives:
(1) To impart an ever-increasing vigour to the Christian life of the faithful;
(2) To adapt more suitably to the needs of our age those institutions which are subject to change;
(3) To foster whatever can promote union among all who believe in Christ;
(4) To strengthen whatever can help to call all mankind into the Church's fold.

Accordingly it sees particularly cogent reasons for undertaking the reform and promotion of the liturgy.

2°. For the liturgy 'through which the work of our redemption is accomplished',[1] most of all in the divine Sacrifice of the Eucharist, is the outstanding means whereby the faithful may express in their lives and manifest to others the mystery of Christ and the real nature of the true Church. The Church is essentially both human and divine, visible but endowed with invisible resources, zealous in action and dedicated to contemplation, present in the world, but as a pilgrim, so constituted that in her the human is directed towards and subordinated to the divine, the visible to the invisible, action to contemplation, and this present world to that city yet to come which we seek.[2] Hence while the liturgy daily builds up those who are within (the Church) into a holy temple of the Lord, into a dwelling-place for God in the Spirit,[3] to the mature measure of the fullness of Christ,[4] at the same time it marvellously strengthens their power to preach Christ and thus show forth the Church to those who are outside (the Church) as a sign lifted up among the nations[5] under which the scattered children of God may be gathered together[6] until there is one fold and one shepherd.[7]

3°. Wherefore the Sacred Council judges that the following principles concerning the promotion and reform of the liturgy should be called to mind, and that practical norms should be established.

Among these principles and norms there are some which can and should be applied both to the Roman rite and also to all the other rites. The practical norms which follow, however, should be taken as applying only to the Roman rite except for those which, in the very nature of things, affect other rites as well.

4°. Finally, in faithful obedience to tradition, the Sacred Council declares that holy Mother Church holds all lawfully recognized rites to be of equal right and dignity: that she wishes to preserve them in the future and to foster them in every way. The Council also desires that, where necessary, the rites be revised carefully in the light of sound tradition, and that they be given new vigour to meet present-day circumstances and needs.

CHAPTER I

GENERAL PRINCIPLES FOR THE RESTORATION AND PROMOTION OF THE SACRED LITURGY

1°. *The Nature of the Sacred Liturgy and its importance in the life of the Church.*

5°. God who 'wills that all men be saved and come to the knowledge

---

1. Secret prayer of 9th Sunday after Pentecost.
2. Cf Hebr. 13:14.
3. Cf Eph. 2:21–22.
4. Cf Eph. 4:13.

5. Cf John 11:12.
6. Cf John 11:52.
7. Cf John 10:16.

of the truth' (1 Tim. 2:4) 'who in many times and various ways spoke of old to the fathers through the prophets' (Hebr. 1:1), when the fullness of time had come sent his Son, the Word made flesh, anointed by the Holy Spirit, to preach the gospel to the poor, to heal the contrite of heart,[8] to be a bodily and spiritual medicine,[9]: the Mediator between God and man.[10] For his humanity united with the Person of the Word was the instrument of our salvation. Therefore, 'in Christ the perfect achievement of our reconciliation came forth and the fullness of divine worship was given to us'.[11]

The wonderful works of God among the people of the Old Testament were but a prelude to the work of Christ Our Lord in redeeming mankind and giving perfect glory to God. He achieved his task principally by the paschal mystery of his blessed passion, resurrection from the dead, and glorious ascension, whereby 'dying, he destroyed our death, and rising, restored our life'.[12] For it was from the side of Christ as he slept the sleep of death upon the cross that there came forth 'the wondrous sacrament of the whole Church'.[13]

6°. Accordingly, just as Christ was sent by the Father so also he sent the apostles, filled with the Holy Spirit. This he did so that they might not only preach the gospel to every creature[14] and proclaim that the Son of God by his death and resurrection had freed us from the power of Satan[15] and from death, and brought us into the Kingdom of his Father, but also that they might carry into effect the work of salvation they preached by means of the Sacrifice and sacraments around which the entire liturgical life revolves. Thus by *Baptism* men are grafted into the paschal mystery of Christ; they die with him, are buried with him, and rise with him,[16] they receive the spirit of adoption as sons 'in which we cry, Abba, Father' (Rom. 8:15), and thus become true adorers such as the Father seeks.[17] In like manner as often as they eat the *Supper of the Lord* they proclaim the death of the Lord until he comes.[18] Wherefore, on the very day of Pentecost when the Church appeared before the world those 'who received the word' of Peter 'were baptized'. And 'they continued steadfastly in the teaching of the apostles and in the communion of the breaking of bread and in prayers . . . praising God and being in

8. Cf Is. 61:1; Luke 4:18.
9. St Ignatius of Antioch, *Ad Ephesios*, 7:2.
10. Cf 1 Tim. 2:5.
11. *Sacramentarium Veronese* (Leonianium).
12. Easter Preface of the Roman Missal.
13. Prayer before Second Lesson of Holy Saturday (Roman Missal, before restoration).
14. Cf Mark 16:15.
15. Cf Acts 26:18.
16. Cf Rom. 6:4; Eph. 2:6; Coloss. 3:1; Tim. 2:11.
17. Cf John 4:23.
18. Cf 1 Cor. 2:26.

favour with all the people' (Acts 2:41–47). From that time onwards the Church has never failed to come together to celebrate the paschal mystery, reading those things 'which were in all the scriptures concerning him' (Luke 24:27), celebrating the Eucharist in which 'the victory and triumph of his death are again made present',[19] and at the same time 'giving thanks to God for his unspeakable gift' (2 Cor. 9:15) in Christ Jesus, 'in praise of his glory' (Eph. 1:12) through the power of the Holy Spirit.

7°. To accomplish so great a work Christ is always present in his Church, especially in her liturgical celebrations. He is present in the Sacrifice of the Mass not only in the person of his minister, 'the same now offering, through the ministry of priests, who formerly offered himself on the cross,[20] but especially in the eucharistic species. By his power he is present in the sacraments so that when anybody baptizes it is really Christ himself who baptizes.[21] He is present in his word since it is he himself who speaks when the holy scriptures are read in the Church. Lastly, he is present when the Church prays and sings, for he has promised 'Where two or three ore gathered together in my name there am I in the midst of them' (Matt. 18:20).

Christ, indeed, always associates the Church with himself in this great work wherein God is perfectly glorified and men are sanctified. The Church is his beloved bride who calls to her Lord, and through him offers worship to the eternal Father.

Rightly, then, the liturgy is regarded as an exercise of the priestly office of Jesus Christ. In the liturgy the sanctification of man is signified by signs perceptible to the senses, and is effected in a way which corresponds to each of these signs. In the liturgy the whole public worship is performed by the Mystical Body of Jesus Christ, that is, by the Head and his members.

From this it follows that every liturgical celebration, because it is an action of Christ the Priest and of his Body, which is the Church, is a sacred action surpassing all others. No other action of the Church can equal its efficacy by the same title and to the same degree.

8°. In the earthly liturgy we take part in a foretaste of that heavenly liturgy which is celebrated in the Holy City of Jerusalem towards which we journey as pilgrims, where Christ is sitting at the right hand of God, Minister of the holy things and of the true tabernacle.[22] With all the warriors of the heavenly army we sing a hymn of the Lord's glory; venerating the memory of the saints, we hope for some part and fellowship with them; we eagerly await the Saviour, Our Lord Jesus Christ, until he our life shall appear and we also will appear with him in glory.[23]

19. Council of Trent, Session 23: Decree on the Holy Eucharist, c. 5.
20. Council of Trent, Session 22: Doctrine on the Holy Sacrifice of the Mass, c. 2.
21. Cf St Augustine, *Tractatus in Ioannem VI*, c. 1, note 7.
22. Cf Apoc. 21:2; Coloss. 3:1; Hebr. 8:2.
23. Cf Philipp. 3:20; Coloss. 3:4.

9°. The sacred liturgy does not exhaust the entire activity of the Church. Before men can come to the liturgy they must be called to faith and to conversion. 'How then are they to call upon him in whom they have not believed? And how are they to believe in him whom they have not heard? And how are they to hear without a preacher? And how are men to preach unless they be sent?' (Rom. 10:14-15).

Therefore the Church announces the good tidings of salvation to those who do not believe, so that all men may know the one true God and Jesus Christ whom he has sent and may be converted from their ways, doing penance.[24] To believers also the Church must ever preach faith and penance; she must prepare them for the sacraments, teach them to observe all that Christ has commanded,[25] and invite them to all the works of charity, piety and the apostolate. For all these works make it clear that Christ's faithful, though not of this world, are to be the lights of the world and are to glorify the Father before men.

10°. Nevertheless the liturgy is the summit towards which the activity of the Church is directed. At the same time it is the fount from which all her power flows. For the object of apostolic works is that all who are made sons of God by faith and baptism should come together to praise God in the midst of his Church, to take part in the Sacrifice and to eat the Lord's Supper.

The liturgy, in its turn, moves the faithful filled with 'the paschal sacraments' to be 'one in holiness'[26]; it prays that 'they hold fast in their lives to what they have grasped by their faith'.[27] The renewal in the Eucharist of the covenant between the Lord and man draws the faithful into the compelling love of Christ and sets them on fire. From the liturgy, therefore, and especially from the Eucharist, grace is poured forth upon us as from a fountain, and the sanctification of men in Christ and the glorification of God to which all other activities of the Church are directed, as towards their end, are achieved in the most efficacious way possible.

11°. But in order that the liturgy may be able to produce its full effects it is necessary that the faithful come to it with proper dispositions, that their minds should be attuned to their voices, and that they should co-operate with heavenly grace lest they receive it in vain.[28] Pastors of souls must, therefore, realize that, when the liturgy is celebrated, something more is required than the laws governing valid and lawful celebration. It is their duty also to ensure that the faithful take part fully aware of what they are doing, actively engaged in the rite and enriched by it.

12°. The spiritual life, however, is not limited solely to participation in the liturgy. The Christian is indeed called to pray with others, but he

24. Cf John 17:3; Luke 24:27; Acts 2:38.
25. Cf Matt. 28:20.
26. Postcommunion for both Masses of Easter Sunday.
27. Collect for Mass of Tuesday of Easter Week.
28. Cf 2 Cor. 6:1.

must also enter into his bedroom to pray to his Father in secret;[29] further-more, according to the teaching of the apostle, he must pray without ceasing.[30] We also learn from the same apostle that we must always carry around in our body the dying of Jesus, so that the life also of Jesus may be made manifest in our mortal flesh.[31] That is why we beg the Lord in the Sacrifice of the Mass that 'receiving the offering of the Spiritual Victim' he may fashion us for himself 'as an eternal gift'.[32]

13°. Popular devotions of the Christian people, provided they conform to the laws and norms of the Church, are to be highly recommended, especially where they are ordered by the Apostolic See.

Devotions proper to individual churches also have a special dignity if they are undertaken by order of the bishops according to customs or books lawfully approved.

But such devotions should be so drawn up that they harmonize with the liturgical seasons, accord with the sacred liturgy, are in some way derived from it and lead the people to it, since in fact the liturgy by its very nature is far superior to any of them.

II.—LITURGICAL INSTRUCTION AND ACTIVE PARTICIPATION

14°. Mother Church earnestly desires that all the faithful should be led to that full, conscious and active participation in liturgical celebrations which is demanded by the very nature of the liturgy, and to which the Christian people 'a chosen race, a royal priesthood, a holy nation, a redeemed people' (1 Peter 2:9, 4–5) have a right and obligation by reason of their baptism.

In the restoration and promotion of the sacred liturgy the full and active participation by all the people is the aim to be considered before all else, for it is the primary and indispensable source from which the faithful are to derive the true Christian spirit. Therefore, pastors of souls must earnestly strive to achieve it in all their pastoral work.

Yet it would be futile to entertain any hope of realizing this unless pastors of souls, in the first place, themselves become fully imbued with the spirit and power of the liturgy and become thoroughly masters oj it. Thus it is absolutely essential, first of all, that steps be taken to ensure the liturgical training of the clergy. For that reason the Sacred Council has decided on the following enactments:

15°. Professors who are appointed to teach liturgy in seminaries, religious houses of studies and theological faculties, must be properly trained for their work in institutes which specialize in this subject.

16°. The study of sacred liturgy is to be ranked among the compulsory

29. Cf Matt. 6:6.
30. Cf 1 Thess. 5:17.
31. Cf 2 Cor. 4:10–11.
32. Secret for Monday of Pentecost Week.

and major courses in seminaries and religious houses of studies. In theological faculties it is to rank among the principal courses. It is to be taught under its theological, historical, spiritual, pastoral and juridical aspects. In addition, professors of other subjects shall take care, especially those who teach dogmatic theology, sacred scripture, spiritual and pastoral theology, that while striving to expound the mystery of Christ and the history of salvation from the angle proper to each of their subjects, they nevertheless clearly set forth the connection between their subject and the liturgy, and the unity which underlies all priestly training.

17°. In seminaries and houses of religious clerics shall be given a liturgical formation in their religious life. For this they will need proper direction so that they may be able to understand the sacred rites and participate in them wholeheartedly, both in the celebration of the sacred mysteries as well as in other popular devotions which are imbued with the spirit of the sacred liturgy. Likewise they must learn to observe the liturgical laws so that life in seminaries and religious institutes may be thoroughly influenced by the liturgical sirit.

18°. Priests, both secular and religous, who are already working in the Lord's vineyard are to be helped by every suitable means to a fuller understanding of what they do when they perform sacred rites, to live the liturgical life and to share it with the faithful entrusted to their care.

19°. With zeal and patience pastors of souls must promote the liturgical instruction of the faithful and also their active participation, both internal and external, taking into account their age, condition, way of life and standard of religious culture. By so doing pastors will be fulfiling one of the chief duties of a faithful dispenser of the mysteries of God, and in this matter they must lead their flock not only by word but also by example.

20°. Transmission of the sacred rites by radio and television, especially in the case of Mass, shall be done with discretion and dignity, under the leadership and direction of a suitable person appointed by the bishops for that office.

THE REFORM OF THE SACRED LITURGY

21°. In order that the Christian people may more certainly derive an abundance of graces from the sacred liturgy, holy Mother Church desires to undertake with great care a general restoration of the liturgy itself. For the liturgy is made up of unchangeable elements divinely instituted, and of elements subject to change. These latter not only may be changed but ought to be changed with the passage of time, if they have suffered from the intrusion of anything out of harmony with the inner nature of the liturgy or have become unsuited to it. In this restoration both texts and rites should be drawn up so as to express more clearly the holy things which they signify. The Christian people, as far as is possible, should be able to understand them with ease and take part in them fully, actively, and as is proper to a community.

Wherefore, the Sacred Council establishes the following general norms:

A: GENERAL NORMS

22°. §1. Regulation of the Sacred Liturgy depends solely on the authority of the Church, that is, on the Apostolic See, and, as laws may determine, on the bishop.

§2. In virtue of power conceded by law, the regulation of the liturgy within certain defined limits belongs also to various kinds of competent territorial bodies of bishops which have been legitimately established.

§3. Therefore no other person, even if he be a priest, may add, remove or change anything in the liturgy on his own authority.

23°. In order that sound tradition be retained, and yet the way remain open to legitimate progress, a careful investigation, based on theological, historical and pastoral grounds, should always be made into each part of the liturgy which is to be revised. Furthermore the general laws governing the structure and meaning of the liturgy must be studied in conjunction with the experience derived from recent liturgical reforms and from the indults to various places.

Finally, there must be no innovations unless the good of the Church genuinely and certainly requires them, and care must be taken that any new forms adopted should in some way grow organically from forms already existing.

Care must be taken, as far as possible, to avoid notable differences between the rites used in adjacent regions.

24° Sacred scripture is of the greatest importance in the celebration of the liturgy. For it is from it that lessons are read and explained in the homily, and psalms are sung. The prayers, collects and liturgical hymns are scriptural in their inspiration, and it is from the scripture that actions and signs derive their meaning. Hence in order to achieve the restoration, progress and adaptation of the sacred liturgy it is essential to promote the warm and living love for sacred scripture, to which the venerable tradition of Eastern and Western rites gives testimony.

25°. The liturgical books are to be revised as soon as possible. Experts are to be employed on this task, and bishops from various parts of the world are to be consulted.

B: NORMS DRAWN FROM THE HIERARCHIC AND COMMUNAL NATURE OF THE LITURGY

26°. Liturgical services are not private functions but are celebrations of the Church which is 'the sacrament of unity', namely, 'the holy people united and arranged under their bishops'.[33]

Therefore, liturgical services pertain to the whole Body of the Church. They manifest it, and have effects upon it. They affect individual members (of the Church) in different ways, according to their differing rank, office and actual participation.

27°. Whenever rites, according to their specific nature, make provision for communal celebration involving the presence and active participation of the faithful, it is to be stressed that in so far as it is possible this method of celebrating them is to be preferred to a celebration that is individual and quasi-private.

This applies with special force to the celebration of Mass (even though every Mass has of itself a public and social nature) and to the administration of the sacraments.

28°. In liturgical celebrations each person, minister or layman, who has an office to perform, should carry out all and only those parts which pertain to his office by the nature of the rite and the principles of the liturgy.

29°. Servers, readers, commentators and members of the choir also exercise a genuine liturgical function. They ought, therefore, to discharge their office with the sincere piety and decorum demanded by so exalted a service and which the people of God rightly expect of them.

Consequently they must all be deeply imbued with the spirit of the liturgy, each in his own measure, and they must be trained to perform their functions in a correct and orderly manner.

30°. To promote active participation the people should be encouraged to take part by means of acclamations, responses, psalms, antiphons, hymns, as well as by actions, gestures and bodily attitudes. And at the proper time a reverent silence should be observed.

31°. The revision of the liturgical books must carefully make provision of rubrics also for the people's parts.

32°. In the liturgy, apart from the distinction arising from liturgical function or sacred orders and the honours due to civil authorities in accordance with liturgical laws, no special exception is to be made for any private persons or classes of persons whether in the ceremonies or by external display.

C: NORMS BASED ON THE DIDACTIC AND PASTORAL NATURE OF THE LITURGY

33°. Although the sacred liturgy is principally the worship of the divine majesty it likewise contains much instruction for the faithful.[34] For in the liturgy God speaks to his people, and Christ is still proclaiming his gospel. And the people reply to God both by song and prayer.

33. St Cyprian 'On the Unity of the Catholic Church', 7; cf Letter 66, n. 8, 3.
34. Cf Council of Trent, Session 22: 'On the Holy Sacrifice of the Mass', c. 8.

Moreover the prayers addressed to God by the priest who, in the person of Christ, preside over the assembly, are said in the name of the entire holy people and of all present. And the visible signs which the sacred liturgy uses to signify invisible divine things have been chosen by Christ or by the Church. Thus not only when things are read 'which were written for our instruction' (Rom. 15:4), but also when the Church prays or sings or acts, the faith of those taking part is nourished, and their minds are raised to God so that they may offer him their reasonable service and more abundantly receive his grace.

Wherefore in the revision of the liturgy the following general norms should be observed.

34°. The rites should be distinguished by a noble simplicity. They should be short, clear and free from useless repetitions. They should be within the people's power of comprehension, and normally should not require much explanation.

35°. That the intimate connection between rite and words may be apparent in the liturgy:

(1) In sacred celebration a fuller, more varied and more suitable reading from sacred scripture should be restored.

(2) Because the sermon is part of the liturgical action the most suitable place should be indicated even in the rubrics as far as the nature of the rite allows. The ministry of preaching is to be fulfilled with the utmost faithfulness and exactitude. The sermon, moreover, should draw its content mainly from scriptural and liturgical sources, as proclaiming God's wonderful works in the history of salvation, or from the mystery of Christ ever made present and operative in us, especially in the celebration of the liturgy.

(3) Instruction which is more explicitly liturgical should also be given in a variety of ways. If necessary, short directives to be spoken by the priest or proper minister should be provided within the rites themselves. But they should occur only at the more suitable moments and should be in prescribed or similar words.

(4) Bible services should be encouraged, especially on the vigils of the more solemn feasts, on some weekdays of Advent and Lent, and on Sundays and Holydays, especially in places where no priest is available. In this case a deacon or some other person authorized by the bishop should preside over the celebration.

36°. §1. The use of the Latin language, with due respect to particular law, is to be preserved in the Latin rites.

§2. But since the use of the vernacular whether in the Mass, the administration of the sacraments or in other parts of the liturgy, may frequently be of great advantage to the people, a wider use may be made of it, especially in readings and directives, in some prayers and chants according to the regulations laid down separately in subsequent chapters.

§3. These norms being observed, it is for the competent territorial ecclesiastical authority mentioned in Article 22 §2, to decide whether, and to what extent, the vernacular language is to be used. Also, where circumstances warrant it, this authority is to consult with bishops of neighbouring regions which have the same language. Their decrees have to be approved or confirmed by the Apostolic See.

§4. Translations from the Latin text into the vernacular for use in the liturgy must be approved by the competent territorial ecclesiastical authority already mentioned.

D: NORMS FOR ADAPTING THE LITURGY TO THE CULTURE AND TRADITIONS OF PEOPLES

37°. Even in the liturgy the Church does not wish to impose a rigid uniformity in matters which do not involve the faith or the good of the whole community. Rather does she respect and foster the external characteristics and talents of the various races and peoples. Anything in these people's way of life which is not indissolubly bound up with superstition and error she studies with sympathy, and, if possible, preserves intact. She sometimes even admits such things into the liturgy itself, provided they harmonize with its true and authentic spirit.

38°. Provided that the substantial unity of the Roman rite is preserved, provision shall also be made, when revising the liturgical books, for legitimate variations and adaptations to different groups, regions and peoples, especially in mission countries. This should be borne in mind when drawing up the rites and determining rubrics.

39°. Within the limits set by the typical editions of the liturgical books it shall be for the competent territorial ecclesiastical authority mentioned in Article 22 §2, to specify adaptations, especially as regards the administration of the sacraments, sacramentals, processions, liturgical language, sacred music and the arts, according, however, to the fundamental norms laid down in this Constitution.

40°. In some places and circumstances, however, an even more radical adaptation of the liturgy may be needed, and this may entail greater difficulties:

Wherefore: (1) the competent territorial ecclesiastical authority mentioned in Article 22 §2, must, in this matter, carefully and prudently consider which elements from the traditions and cultures of individual peoples may appropriately be admitted into divine worship. Adaptations which are considered useful or necessary should then be submitted to the Holy See, by whose consent they may be introduced.

(2) To ensure that adaptations may be made with all the circumspection necessary, the Apostolic See will grant power to this same territorial ecclesiastical authority to permit and to direct, as the case requires, the necessary preliminary experiments over

a determined period of time among certain groups suitable for the purpose.

(3) Because liturgical laws often involve special difficulties with respect to adaptation, especially in mission lands, men who are experts in the matters in question must be employed to formulate them.

E: PROMOTION OF THE LITURGICAL LIFE IN DIOCESE AND PARISH

41°. The bishop is to be considered as the High Priest of his flock from whom the life in Christ of his faithful is in some way derived and upon whom it in some way depends.

Therefore all should hold in the greatest esteem the liturgical life of the diocese centred around the bishop, especially in his cathedral church. They must be convinced that the pre-eminent manifestation of the Church consists in the full, active participation of all God's holy people in these liturgical celebrations, especially in the same Eucharist, in a single prayer, at one altar, at which the bishop presides surrounded by his college of priests and by his ministers.[35]

42°. But as it is impossible for the bishop always and everywhere to preside over the whole flock in his church he must of necessity establish groupings of the faithful; and among these the parishes, set up locally under a pastor who takes the place of the bishop, are the most important, for in some way they represent the visible Church constituted throughout the world.

Therefore the liturgical life of the parish and its relation to the bishop must be fostered in their thought and practice among the faithful and clergy. Efforts must also be made to encourage a sense of community within the parish, above all in the common celebration of the Sunday Mass.

F: THE PROMOTION OF PASTORAL LITURGICAL ACTION

43°. Zeal for the promotion and restoration of the sacred liturgy is rightly held to be a sign of the providential dispositions of God in our time, and as a movement of the Holy Spirit in his Church. It is today a distinguishing mark of the life of the Church, and, indeed, of the whole tenor of contemporary religious thought and action.

Therefore, so that this pastoral liturgical action may become still more vigorous in the Church the sacred Council decrees:

44°. It is desirable that the competent territorial ecclesiastical authority mentioned in Article 22 §2, set up a liturgical commission to be assisted by experts in liturgical science, sacred music, art and pastoral practice. So far as is possible the commission should be aided by some kind of Institute for Pastoral Liturgy, consisting of persons who are eminent in

---

35. Cf St Ignatius of Antioch: Ad Magn. 7; Ad Phil. 4; Ad Smyrn. 8.

these matters, not excluding laymen, if circumstances so demand. It will be the task of this commission, under the direction of the above-mentioned competent territorial ecclesiastical authority (*vide* Article 22 §2), to regulate pastoral liturgical action throughout the territory, and to promote studies and necessary experiments whenever there is question of adaptations to be proposed to the Holy See.

45°. For the same reason every diocese is to have a commission on the sacred liturgy, under the direction of the bishop, for promoting the liturgical apostolate.

Sometimes it may be expedient that several dioceses should form between them one single commission which will be able to promote the liturgy by common consultation.

46°. In addition to the commission on sacred liturgy every diocese, as far as possible, should have commissions for sacred music and sacred art.

These three commissions must work in the closest collaboration. Indeed it will often be best to join the three of them in one single commission.

CHAPTER II

THE MOST SACRED MYSTERY OF THE EUCHARIST

47°. At the Last Supper, on the night he was betrayed, our Saviour instituted the eucharistic sacrifice of his Body and Blood. This he did in order to perpetuate the sacrifice of the Cross throughout the ages until he should come again, and so to entrust to his beloved spouse, the Church, a memorial of his death and resurrection: a sacrament of love, a sign of unity, a bond of charity,[36] a paschal banquet in which Christ is consumed, the mind is filled with grace, and a pledge of future glory is given to us.[37]

48°. The Church, therefore, earnestly desires that Christ's faithful, when present at this mystery of faith, should not be there as strangers or silent spectators. On the contrary, through a good understanding of the rites and prayers they should take part in the sacred action, conscious of what they are doing, with devotion and full collaboration. They should be instructed by God's word, and be nourished at the table of the Lord's Body. They should give thanks to God. Offering the immaculate victim, not only through the hands of the priest but also together with him, they should learn to offer themselves. Through Christ, the Mediator,[38] they should be drawn day by day into ever more perfect union with God and each other, so that finally God may be all in all.

49°. For this reason the sacred Council having in mind those Masses

36. Cf St Augustine, 'Tractatus in Ioannis Evangelium', c. 6, n. 13.
37. Roman Breviary: Feast of Corpus Christi: 2nd Vesp. Antiph. to Magnificat.
38. Cf St Cyril of Alexandria: Commentary on Gospel of St John, bk. 11, c. 11–12.

which are celebrated with the faithful assisting, especially on Sundays and holydays of obligation, has made the following decrees so that the sacrifice of the Mass, even in the ritual forms (of its celebration) may have full pastoral efficacy.

DECREES

50°. The rite of the Mass is to be revised in such a way that the intrinsic nature and purpose of its several parts, as well as the connection between them, may be more clearly manifested, and that devout and active participation by the faithful may be more easily achieved.

For this purpose the rites are to be simplified, due care being taken to preserve their substance. Parts which with the passage of time came to be duplicated, or were added with little advantage, are to be omitted. Other parts which suffered loss through accidents of history are to be restored to the vigour they had in the days of the holy Fathers, as may seem useful or necessary.

51°. The treasures of the Bible are to be opened up more lavishly so that a richer fare may be provided for the faithful at the table of God's word. Thus a more representative part of the sacred scriptures will be read to the people in the course of a prescribed number of years.

52°. By means of the homily the mysteries of the faith and the guiding principles of the Christian life are expounded from the sacred text during the course of the liturgical year. The homily, therefore, is to be highly esteemed as part of the liturgy itself. In fact at those Masses which are celebrated on Sundays and holydays of obligation, with the people assisting, it should not be omitted except for a serious reason.

53°. The 'common prayer' or 'prayer of the faithful' is to be restored after the gospel and homily, especially on Sundays and holydays of obligation. By this prayer in which the people are to take part, intercession will be made for holy Church, for the civil authorities, for those oppressed by various needs, for all mankind, and for the salvation of the entire world.[39]

54°. A suitable place may be found for the vernacular in Masses which are celebrated with the people, especially in the readings and 'the common prayer', and also, as local conditions may warrant, in those parts which pertain to the people, according to the rules laid down in Article 36 of this Constitution.

Nevertheless steps should be taken so that the faithful may also be able to say or sing together in Latin those parts of the Ordinary of the Mass which pertain to them.

Whenever a more extended use of the vernacular in the Mass seems desirable the regulation laid down in Article 40 of this Constitution is to be observed.

39. Cf 1 Tim. 2:1–2.

55°. That more perfect form of participation in the Mass whereby the faithful, after the priest's communion, receive the Lord's Body from the same sacrifice, is warmly recommended.

The dogmatic principles which were laid down by the Council of Trent remaining intact,[40] communion under both kinds may be granted when the bishops think fit, not only to clerics and religious but also to the laity, in cases to be determined by the Apostolic See. For example,

To the newly ordained in the Mass of their ordination;

To the newly professed in the Mass of their religious profession;

To the newly baptized in the Mass which follows their baptism.

56°. The two parts which in a sense go to make up the Mass, viz. the liturgy of the word and the eucharistic liturgy, are so closely connected with each other that they form but one single act of worship. Accordingly the sacred Synod strongly urges pastors of souls that, when instructing the faithful, they insistently teach them to take their part in the entire Mass, especially on Sundays and holydays of obligation.

57°. §1. Concelebration whereby the unity of the priesthood is appropriately manifested has remained in use to this day in the Church both in the East and in the West. For this reason it has seemed good to the Council to extend permission for concelebration to the following cases:

    1. (a) On the Thursday of the Lord's Supper, not only at the Mass of the Chrism, but also at the evening Mass.

       (b) At Masses during Councils, Bishops' Conferences and Synods.

       (c) At the Mass for the Blessing of an abbot.

    2. Also, with permission of the Ordinary, to whom it belongs to decide whether concelebration is opportune:

       (a) at conventual Mass, and at the principal Mass in churches when the needs of the faithful do not require that all the priests available should celebrate individually;

       (b) at Mass celebrated at any kind of priests' meetings whether the priests be secular or religious.

  §2. (1) The regulation, however, of the discipline of concelebration in the diocese pertains to the bishop.

      (2) Each priest shall always retain his right to celebrate Mass individually, though not at the same time in the same church as a Mass of concelebration nor on the Thursday of the Lord's Supper.

58°. A new rite for concelebration is to be drawn up and inserted into the Pontifical and into the Roman Missal.

40. Council of Trent, Session 21: 'On Communion under both Species', c. 1–3.

CHAPTER III

THE OTHER SACRAMENTS AND THE SACRAMENTALS

59°. The purpose of the sacraments is to sanctify men, to build up the body of Christ, and, finally, to give worship to God. Because they are signs they also instruct. They not only presuppose faith, but by words and objects they also strengthen and express it. That is why they are called 'sacraments of faith'. They do, indeed, confer grace, but, in addition, the very act of celebrating them most effectively disposes the faithful to receive this grace in a fruitful manner, to worship God duly, and to practise charity.

It is, therefore, of the greatest importance that the faithful should easily understand the sacramental signs, and should frequent with the greatest eagerness those sacraments which were instituted to nourish the Christian life.

60°. Holy Mother Church has, moreover, instituted sacramentals. These are sacred signs which bear a resemblance to the sacraments. They signify effects, particularly of a spiritual nature, which are obtained through the Church's intercession. By them men are disposed to receive the chief effect of the sacraments, and various occasions in life are rendered holy.

61°. Thus, for well-disposed members of the faithful the liturgy of the sacraments and sacramentals sanctifies almost every event of their lives with the divine grace which flows from the paschal mystery of the Passion, Death and Resurrection of Christ. From this source all sacraments and sacramentals draw their power. There is scarcely any proper use of material things which cannot thus be directed towards the sanctification of men and the praise of God.

62°. With the passage of time, however, there have crept into the rites of the sacraments and sacramentals certain features which have rendered their nature and purpose far from clear to the people of today. Hence some changes are necessary to adapt them to present-day needs. For that reason the sacred Council decrees as follows concerning their revision:

63°. Because the use of the vernacular in the administration of the sacraments and sacramentals can often be of very great help to the people this use is to be extended according to the following norms:

(a) In the administration of the sacraments and sacramentals the vernacular may be used according to the norm of Article 36.

(b) The competent territorial ecclesiastical authority designated in Article 22 §2 of this Constitution shall forthwith prepare, in accordance with the new edition of the Roman Ritual, local rituals adapted linguistically and otherwise to the needs of the different regions. These rituals, on authentication by the Apostolic See, are to be followed in the regions in question. But in drawing up those rituals or particular collections of rites the instructions prefixed to the individual rites in the Roman Ritual, whether they be pastoral and rubrical or whether they have a special social import, shall not be omitted.

64°. The catechumenate for adults, comprising several distinct steps, is to be restored and brought into use at the discretion of the local Ordinary. By this means the time of the catechumenate, which is intended as a period of suitable instruction, may be sanctified by sacred rites to be celebrated at successive intervals of time.

65°. In mission countries, in addition to those things based on the Christian tradition, those elements of initiation rites may be admitted which are already in use among some peoples in so far as they can be adapted to the Christian ritual in accordance with Articles 37–40 of this Constitution.

66°. Both rites for the baptism of adults are to be revised, not only the simpler rite but also, taking into consideration the restored catechumenate, the more solemn rite. A special Mass 'For the conferring of Baptism' is to be inserted into the Roman Missal.

67°. The rite for the baptism of infants is to be revised, and adapted to the fact that those to be baptized are indeed infants. The roles of parents and godparents, and also their duties, should be brought out more clearly in the rite itself.

68°. The baptismal rite should contain variants, to be used at the discretion of the local Ordinary, when a large number are to be baptized. Likewise a shorter *Ordo* is to be drawn up, especially in mission countries which catechists, and also the faithful in general when there is danger of death, may use when neither priest nor deacon is available.

69°. In place of the rite called 'Order of supplying what was omitted in the baptism of an infant' a new rite is to be drawn up. This rite should indicate more fittingly and clearly that the infant baptized by the short rite has already been received into the Church.

So also a new rite is to be drawn up for converts who have already been validly baptized. It should indicate that they are now admitted to communion with the Church.

70°. Baptismal water, outside of paschal time, may be blessed within the rite of Baptism itself by an approved shorter formula.

71°. The rite of Confirmation is to be revised also so that the intimate connection of this sacrament with the whole of the Christian initiation may more clearly appear. For this reason the renewal of baptismal promises should fittingly precede the reception of this sacrament.

Confirmation may be conferred within Mass when convenient. For conferring outside Mass, a formula introducing the rite should be drawn up.

72°. The rite and formulae of Penance are to be revised so that they more clearly express both the nature and effect of the sacrament.

73°. 'Extreme Unction' which may also and more fittingly be called 'Anointing of the Sick', is not a sacrament for those only who are at the point of death. Hence, as soon as anyone of the faithful begins to be in danger of death from sickness or old age the fitting time for him to receive this sacrament has certainly already arrived.

74°. In addition to the separate rites for Anointing of the Sick and for Viaticum, a continuous rite shall be prepared according to which the sick man is anointed after he has made his confession and before he receives Viaticum.

75°. The number of the anointings is to be adapted to the occasion, and the prayers which belong to the rite of anointing are to be revised so as to correspond to the varying conditions of the sick who receive the sacrament.

76°. Both the ceremonies and texts of the ordination rites are to be revised. The addresses given by the bishop at the beginning of each ordination or consecration may be in the vernacular.

In the consecration of a bishop the laying on of hands may be done by all the bishops present.

77°. The marriage rite now found in the Roman Ritual is to be revised and enriched in such a way that the grace of the sacrament is more clearly signified and the duties of the spouses taught.

'If any regions are wont to use other praiseworthy customs and ceremonies when celebrating the sacrament of Matrimony the sacred Synod earnestly desires that these be certainly retained'.[41]

Moreover, the competent territorial ecclesiastical authority designated in Article 22 §2 of this Constitution is free to draw up its own rite suited to the usages of places and peoples, according to the provisions of Article 63. But the rite must always conform to the law that the priest assisting at the marriage must ask for and obtain the consent of the contracting parties.

78°. Matrimony is normally to be celebrated within the Mass after the reading of the gospel and the homily and before 'the prayer of the faithful'. The prayer for the bride, duly amended to remind both spouses of their equal obligation of mutual fidelity, may be said in the vernacular.

But if the sacrament of Matrimony is celebrated apart from Mass the epistle and gospel from the nuptial Mass are to be read at the beginning of the rite, and the blessing should always be given to the spouses.

79°. The sacramentals are to be revised, account being taken of the primary principle of enabling the faithful to participate intelligently, actively and easily. The circumstances of our times must also be considered. When rituals are being revised as laid down in Article 63 new sacramentals may also be added as necessity requires.

Reserved blessings shall be very few. Reservations shall be in favour only of bishops or ordinaries.

Let provision be made that some sacramentals, at least in special

41. Council of Trent, Session 24: 'On Reform', c. 1. Cf Roman Ritual Title 8, c. 2, n. 6.

circumstances and at the discretion of the ordinary, may be administered by qualified lay persons.

80°. The rite of the Consecration of Virgins contained in the Roman Pontifical is to be revised.

Moreover the rite of religious profession and renewal of vows shall be drawn up in order to achieve greater unity, sobriety and dignity. Apart from any particular law this rite should be adopted by those who make their profession or renewal of vows within the Mass.

81°. Funeral rites should express more clearly the paschal character of Christian death, and should correspond more closely to the circumstances and traditions found in various regions. This also applies to the liturgical colour to be used.

82°. The rite for the burial of infants is to be revised, and a special Mass for the occasion should be provided.

CHAPTER IV

THE DIVINE OFFICE

83°. Jesus Christ, High Priest of the New and Eternal Covenant, taking human nature, introduced into this earthly exile the hymn which is sung throughout all ages in the heavenly dwelling-places. He joins the entire community of mankind to himself, associating it with himself in singing this divine song of praise.

For he continues his priestly work through his Church which is ceaselessly engaged in praising the Lord in interceding for the salvation of the entire world. This she does not only by celebrating the Eucharist but also in other ways, especially by praying the divine office.

84°. By tradition which goes back to the early Christian times the divine office is so devised that the whole course of the day and night is made holy by the praise of God. Therefore when this wonderful song of praise is rightly performed by priests and others who are deputed for this purpose by the Church's ordinance, or by the faithful praying together with the priest in the approved form, then it is truly the voice of the Bride herself addressed to her Spouse. It is the very prayer which Christ himself together with his body addresses to the Father.

85°. Hence all who render this service are not only fulfilling a duty of the Church but are sharing also in the greatest honour of Christ's spouse, for by offering these praises to God they are standing before God's throne in the name of the Church, their Mother.

86°. Priests who are engaged in the sacred pastoral ministry will offer the praises of the hours with greater fervour the more vividly they realize that they must heed St Paul's exhortation 'Pray without ceasing' (1 Thess. 5:17). For the work in which they labour will effect nothing and bring forth no fruit except through the power of the Lord who said 'Without me you can do nothing' (John 15:5). That is why the apostles when instituting deacons said: 'We will devote ourselves to prayer and to the ministry of the word' (Acts 6:4).

87°. In order that the divine office may be better and more perfectly prayed, whether by priests or by other members of the Church, in existing circumstances, the sacred Council, carrying further the restoration so happily begun by the Apostolic See, decrees as follows concerning the office of the Roman rite.

88°. Since the purpose of the office is to sanctify the day the traditional sequence of the hours is to be restored so that, as far as possible, they may be genuinely related to the time of the day (when they are prayed). At the same time account must be taken of the conditions of modern life in which those especially who are engaged in apostolic work must live.

89°. Therefore, in the revision of the office these norms are to be observed:

(a) By the venerable tradition of the universal Church, Lauds as morning prayers, and Vespers as evening prayer, are the two hinges on which the daily office turns. They must be considered as the chief hours and are to be celebrated as such.

(b) Compline is to be drawn up so as suitably to mark the close of the day.

(c) The hour called Matins, although it should retain the character of nocturnal prayer when recited in choir, shall be so adapted that it may be recited at any hour of the day, and it shall be made up of fewer psalms and longer readings.

(d) The hour of Prime is to be suppressed.

(e) In choir the minor hours of Terce, Sect and None are to be observed. Outside of choir it will be lawful to select any one of the three most suited to the time of the day.

90°. Now since the divine office, because it is the public prayer of the Church, should be a source of piety and a nourishment for personal prayer, priests and others who take part in the divine office are earnestly exhorted in the Lord to attune their minds to their voices when praying it. The better to accomplish this let them take steps to improve their understanding of the liturgy, and of the Bible, especially of the psalms.

In carrying out the revision the venerable treasure of the Roman office should be so adapted that all those to whom it is handed on may more extensively and easily draw profit from it.

91°. So that it may really be possible in practice to observe the course of the hours proposed in Article 89, the psalms are no longer to be distributed throughout one week but through a longer period of time.

The task of revising the psalter, already happily begun, is to be finished as soon as possible. It shall take into account the style of Christian Latin, the liturgical use of the psalms even when sung, and the entire tradition of the Latin Church.

92°. As regards the readings, the following points shall be observed:

(a) Readings from sacred scripture shall be so arranged that the riches of the divine word may be easily accessible in more abundant measure.

(b) Readings taken from the works of the fathers, doctors and ecclesiastical writers shall be better selected.

(c) The accounts of the martyrdom or lives of the saints are to accord with the facts of history.

93°. Hymns are to be restored to their original form, as far as may be desirable. Whatever savours of mythology or does not accord with Christian piety is to be removed or changed. Also, as occasion may warrant, other selections are to be made from the treasury of hymns.

94°. So that the day may be truly sanctified and that the hours themselves may be recited with spiritual advantage, it is best that each of them be prayed at the time which corresponds most closely with its true canonical time.

95°. Communities obliged to choral office are bound to celebrate the office in choir each day in addition to the conventual Mass. In particular:

(a) Orders of canons, monks and nuns, and of other regulars bound by law or constitutions to choral office, must say the entire office;

*b\ Cathedral or collegiate chapters are bound to recite those parts of the office imposed on them by general or particular law;

(c) All members of the above communities who are in major orders or who are solemnly professed, except for lay brothers, are bound to recite individually those canonical hours which they do not pray in choir.

96°. Clerics not bound to office in choir, if they are in major orders, are bound to pray the entire office every day, either in common or individually, as laid down in Article 89.

97°. Appropriate instances are to be defined in the rubrics in which a liturgical service may be substituted for the divine office.

In particular cases, and for a just cause, ordinaries can dispense their subjects, wholly or in part, from the obligation of reciting the divine office, or they may commute the obligation.

98°. Members of any institute dedicated to acquiring perfection who, according to their constitutions, are to recite some parts of the divine office, are thereby performing the public prayer of the Church.

They, also, perform the public prayer of the Church if, in virtue of the constitutions, they recite any short office, provided it is drawn up after the pattern of the divine office, and is duly approved.

99°. Since the divine office is the voice of the Church, that is, of the whole mystical body publicly praising God, it is recommended that clerics who are not obliged to attend office in choir, especially priests who live together or who assemble for any purpose, should pray at least some part of the divine office in common.

All who pray the divine office, whether in choir or in common, should fulfil the task entrusted to them as perfectly as possible. This refers not only to the internal devotion of mind but also to the external manner of celebration.

It is, moreover, fitting that the office both in choir and in common, be sung when possible.

100°. Pastors of souls should see to it that the principal hours, especially Vespers, are celebrated in common in church on Sundays and the more solemn feasts. The laity, too, are encouraged to recite the divine office, either with the priests, or among themselves, or even individually.

101°. §1. In accordance with the age-old tradition of the Latin rite, the Latin language is to be retained by clerics in the divine office. But in individual cases the ordinary has the power of granting the use of a vernacular translation to those clerics for whom the use of Latin constitutes a grave obstacle to their praying the office properly. The vernacular version, however, must be one that is drawn up in accordance with the provisions of Article 36.

§2. In the case of nuns, and members of institutes dedicated to acquiring perfection, female or non-clerical male, the competent superior has the power to grant the use of the vernacular in the celebration of the divine office, even in choir. The vernacular version, however, must be one that is approved.

§3. Any cleric bound to the divine office fulfils his obligation if he prays the office in the vernacular together with a group of the faithful or with those mentioned in §2, above, provided that the text of the translation is approved.

CHAPTER V

THE LITURGICAL YEAR

102°. Holy Mother Church is conscious that she must celebrate the saving work of her divine Spouse by devoutly recalling it on certain days throughout the course of the year. Every week on the day which she has called the Lord's Day she keeps the memory of the Lord's resurrection which she also celebrates once a year, together with his blessed passion, in the most solemn festival of Easter.

Moreover within the cycle of the year she unfolds the whole mystery of Christ from the incarnation and nativity to the ascension, Pentecost and the expectation of the blessed hope of the coming of the Lord.

Thus recalling the mysteries of the redemption she opens up to the faithful the riches of her Lord's powers and merits, so that these are in some way made present for all time, and they who lay hold of them are filled with saving grace.

103°. In celebrating this annual cycle of the mysteries of Christ, holy Church honours with especial love the Blessed Mary, Mother of God, who is joined by an inseparable bond to the saving work of her Son. In her the Church admires and holds aloft the most excellent fruit of redemption, and joyfully contemplates, as in a faultless image, that which she herself desires and hopes wholly to be.

104°. The Church has also included in the annual cycle memorial days of the martyrs and other saints. Raised up to perfection by the manifold grace of God and already in possession of eternal salvation, they sing God's perfect praise in heaven and make intercession for us. By celebrating the passage of these saints from earth to heaven the Church proclaims the paschal mystery achieved in the saints who have suffered and been glorified with Christ. She proposes them to the faithful as examples who draw all men to the Father through Christ, and through their merits she begs for God's favours.

105°. Finally, in the various seasons of the year and according to her traditional discipline, the Church completes the formation of the faithful by means of pious practices for soul and body, by instruction, prayer, and works of penance and mercy.

Accordingly the sacred Council has seen fit to decree as follows:

106°. By a tradition handed down from the apostles, which took its origin from the very day of Christ's resurrection, the Church celebrates the paschal mystery every eighth day, which day is appropriately called the Lord's Day or Sunday. For on this day Christ's faithful should come together into one place so that hearing the word of God and taking part in the Eucharist, they may call to mind the passion, resurrection and glory of the Lord Jesus, and may give thanks to God who 'has begotten them again, through the resurrection of Christ from the dead, unto a living hope' (1 Peter 1:3). The the Lord's Day is the original feastday, and it should be proposed to the faithful and taught to them so that it may become in fact a day of joy and of freedom from work. Other celebrations, unless they be truly of the greatest importance, shall not have precedence over Sunday, which is the foundation and kernel of the whole liturgical year.

107°. The liturgical year is to be revised so that the traditional customs and discipline of the sacred seasons shall be preserved or restored to suit the conditions of modern times. Their specific character is to be retained so that they duly nourish the piety of the faithful who celebrate the mysteries of the Christian redemption and, above all, the paschal mystery. If certain adaptations are necessary because of local conditions, they are to be made in accordance with the provisions of Articles 39 and 40.

108°. The minds of the faithful should be directed primarily towards the feasts of the Lord whereby the mysteries of salvation are celebrated throughout the year. Then the proper time shall be given due preference over the feasts of the saints so that the entire cycle of the mysteries of salvation may be suitably recalled.

109°. The season of Lent has a twofold character. By recalling or preparing for baptism and by penance, it disposes the faithful who more diligently hear the word of God and devote themselves to prayer, to celebrate the paschal mystery. This twofold character is to be brought into greater prominence both in the liturgy and by liturgical catechesis. Hence:

   (*a*) More use is to be made of the baptismal features which are proper to the Lenten liturgy. Some of them which were part of an earlier tradition are to be restored as may seem good.
   (*b*) The same may be said of the penitential elements. But instruction, as well as pointing out social consequences of sin, must impress on the minds of the faithful the distinctive character of penance as a detestation of sin because it is an offence against God. The role of the Church in penitential practices is not to be passed over, and prayers for sinners should be earnestly requested.

110°. During Lent penance should be not only internal and individual but also external and social. The practice of penance should be fostered in ways that are possible in our times and in different regions, and according to the circumstances of the faithful. It should be encouraged by the authorities mentioned in Article 22.

But the paschal fast must be kept sacred. Let it be celebrated everywhere on Good Friday, and where possible be prolonged throughout Holy Saturday so that the joys of the Sunday of the resurrection may be attained with uplifted and clear mind.

111°. The saints have been traditionally honoured in the Church, and their authentic relics and images held in veneration. For the feasts of the saints proclaim the wonderful works of Christ in his servants and displays to the faithful fitting examples for their imitation.

Lest the feasts of the saints should take precedence over the feasts which commemorate the very mysteries of salvation, many of them should be left to be celebrated by a particular Church, or nation, or family of religious. Only those should be extended to the universal Church which commemorate saints who are truly of universal importance.

CHAPTER VI

SACRED MUSIC

112°. The musical tradition of the universal Church is a treasure of inestimable value, greater even than that of any other art. The main reasons for this pre-eminence is, that as sacred song unites to the words, it forms a necessary or integral part of the solemn liturgy.

Sacred scripture, indeed, has bestowed praise upon sacred song.[42] So have the holy Fathers and the Roman pontiffs who in more recent times, led by St Pius X, have explained more precisely the ministerial function supplied by sacred music in the service of the Lord.

42. Cf Eph. 5:19; Coloss. 3:16.

Therefore sacred music is to be considered the more holy in proportion as it is more closely connected with the liturgical action, whether it adds delight to prayer, fosters unity of minds, or confers greater solemnity upon the sacred rites. The Church, indeed, approves of all forms of true art which have the required qualities, and admits them into divine worship.

Accordingly, the sacred Council, keeping to the norms and precepts of ecclesiastical tradition and discipline and having regard to the purpose of sacred music which is the glory of God and the sanctification of the faithful, decrees as follows:

113°. Liturgical worship is given a more noble form when the divine offices are celebrated solemnly in song with the assistance of sacred ministers and the active participation of the people.

As regards the language to be used the provisions of Article 36 are to be observed. For the sacraments, Article 63, and for the divine office, Article 101.

114°. The treasure of sacred music is to be preserved and fostered with great care. Choirs must be diligently promoted especially in cathedral churches. Bishops and other pastors of souls must take great care to ensure that whenever the sacred action is to be celebrated with song, the whole body of the faithful may be able to contribute that active participation which is rightly theirs, as laid down in Articles 28 and 30.

115°. Great importance is to be attached to the teaching and practice of music in seminaries, in the novitiates and houses of studies of religious of both sexes, and also in other Catholic institutions and schools. To impart this instruction teachers are to be carefully trained and put in charge of the teaching of sacred music.

It is desirable also that higher institutes of sacred music be established whenever possible.

Composers and singers, especially boys, must also be given a genuine liturgical training.

116°. The Church recognizes Gregorian chant as being specially suited to the Roman liturgy. Therefore, other things being equal, it should be given pride of place in liturgical services.

Other kinds of sacred music, especially polyphony, are by no means excluded from liturgical celebrations so long as they accord with the spirit of the liturgical action as laid down in Article 30.

117°. The typical edition of the books of Gregorian chant is to be compiled. In addition a more critical edition is to be prepared of those books already published since the restoration by St Pius X.

It is desirable also that an edition be prepared containing simpler melodies for use in smaller churches.

118°. Religious singing by the faithful is to be skilfully fostered so that in devotions and sacred exercises as well as in liturgical services, the voices of the faithful may ring out according to the norms and requirements of the rubrics.

119°. In certain countries, especially in mission lands, there are people who have their own musical tradition, and this plays a great part in their religious and social life. For this reason due importance is to be attached to their music and a suitable place is to be given to it not only in forming their attitude towards religion but also in adapting worship to their native genius, as indicated in Articles 39 and 40.

Therefore, in the musical training of missionaries great care should be taken to see that they become competent in promoting the traditional music of those peoples both in the schools and in sacred services, as far as may be practicable.

120°. The pipe organ is to be held in high esteem in the Latin Church for it is the traditional musical instrument which adds a wonderful splendour to the Church's ceremonies, and powerfully lifts up men's minds to God and higher things.

But other instruments also may be admitted for use in divine worship, with the approval and consent of the competent territorial authority as laid down in Articles 22 §2, 37 and 40. This may be done, however, only on condition that the instruments are suitable or can be made suitable for sacred use; that they accord with the dignity of the temple, and that they truly contribute to the edification of the faithful.

121°. Composers, filled with the Christian spirit, should feel that their vocation is to cultivate sacred music and increase its store of treasures.

Let them produce compositions which have the qualities proper to genuine sacred music, not confining themselves to those which can be sung only by large choirs but providing also compositions suitable for smaller choirs and for encouraging the active participation of the whole congregation.

The texts intended to be sung must always be in conformity with Catholic doctrine. Indeed they should be drawn chiefly from the sacred scripture and from liturgical sources.

CHAPTER VII

SACRED ART AND SACRED FURNISHINGS

122°. Very rightly the fine arts are considered to rank among the noblest activities of man's genius, and this applies especially to religious art, and to its highest achievement which is sacred art. The arts by their very nature tend towards the infinite divine beauty which they try to express in some way by the works of human hands. They attain their purpose of promoting God's praise and glory in proportion as they are directed the more exclusively to the single aim of turning men's minds devoutly towards God.

For that reason Holy Mother Church has always been the friend of the fine arts, and has ever sought their noble help with the special objective that all things set apart for use in divine worship should be worthy, becoming and beautiful, signs and symbols of things supernatural. And for this purpose she has trained artists. In fact the Church has, with good reason, always claimed the right to pass judgment on the arts, deciding which of the works of artists are in accordance with faith, piety, and cherished traditional laws, and are to be considered suitable for sacred use.

The Church has been particularly careful to see that sacred furnishing should worthily and beautifully serve the dignity of worship. She has admitted changes in material, style or ornamentation prompted by the progress of technical arts with the passage of time.

Wherefore it has pleased the Fathers to issue the following decrees on these matters.

123°. The Church has not adopted any particular style of art as her own. She has admitted styles from every period, according to the natural talents and circumstances of peoples and the needs of the various rites. Thus in the course of the centuries she has brought into existence a treasury of art which must be preserved with every care. The art of our own times coming from every race and country shall also be given free scope in the Church, provided that it adorns sacred buildings and holy rites with due reverence and honour. Thus it is enabled to join its voice to that wonderful chorus of praise in honour of the Catholic faith sung by great men in past ages.

124°. Ordinaries are to take care that in the encouragement and favour they show to art which is truly sacred they should seek for noble beauty rather than sumptuous display. The same principle is to apply also as regards sacred vestments and ornaments.

Let Ordinaries see to it that works of art which are repugnant to faith, morals and Christian piety, and which offend true religious sense either by depraved forms or through lack of artistic merit, or because of mediocrity or pretence, shall be removed from the house of God and from other sacred places.

And when churches are to be built let great care be taken that they be suitable for the celebration of liturgical services and for the active participation of the faithful.

125°. The practice of placing sacred images in churches so that they be venerated by the faithful is to be maintained. Nevertheless their number should be moderate and their relative positions should reflect right order. For otherwise they may create confusion among the Christian people and foster devotion of doubtful orthodoxy.

126°. When passing judgment on works of art local ordinaries shall hear the opinion of the diocesan commission on sacred art and, if necessary, the opinions of others who are experts, and the commissions mentioned in Articles 44, 45 and 46.

Ordinaries must be very careful to see that sacred furnishing and works of value are not disposed of or destroyed, for they are the ornaments of God's house.

127°. Bishops, either personally or through suitable priests who are gifted with a knowledge and love of art, should have a special concern for artists so as to imbue them with the spirit of sacred art and of the sacred liturgy.

It is also desirable that schools or academies of sacred art should be established in those parts of the world where they would be useful for the training of artists.

All artists who, prompted by their talents, desire to serve God's glory in holy Church should ever remember that they are engaged in a kind of sacred imitation of God the Creator: that they are concerned with works destined to be used in Catholic worship, for the edification of the faithful and to foster their piety and religious formation.

128°. The canons and ecclesiastical statutes which govern the provision of external things which pertain to sacred worship should as soon as possible be revised together with the liturgical books in accordance with Article 25. These laws refer especially to the worthy and well-planned construction of sacred buildings, the shape and construction of altars, the nobility, placing and safety of the eucharistic tabernacle, the dignity and suitability of the baptistry, the proper ordering of sacred images, and the scheme of decoration and embellishment. Laws which seem less suited to the reformed liturgy should be amended or abolished. Those which are helpful are to be retained, or introduced if lacking.

In this matter, especially as regards the material and form of sacred furnishing and vestments, in accordance with Article 22 of this Constitution, powers are given to territorial episcopal conferences to adapt such things to the needs and customs of their different regions.

129°. During their philosophical and theological studies, clerics are to be taught about the history and development of sacred art, and about the sound principles which govern the production of its works. Thus they will be able to appreciate and preserve the Church's venerable monuments, and be able to aid by good advice artists who are engaged in producing works of art.

130°. It is fitting that the use of pontificals be reserved to those ecclesiastical persons who have episcopal rank or some particular jurisdiction.

APPENDIX

A DECLARATION OF THE SECOND VATICAN ECUMENICAL COUNCIL ON
Revision of the Calendar

The Second Sacred Vatican Ecumenical Council, recognizing the importance of the wishes expressed by many concerning the assignment of the feast of Easter to a fixed Sunday and concerning an unchanging calendar, having carefully considered the results that could follow from the introduction of a new calendar, declares as follows:

1°. The sacred Council is not opposed to assigning the feast of Easter to a fixed Sunday in the Gregorian Calendar provided those whom it may concern give their assent, especially the brethren who are not in communion with the Apostolic See.

2°. The sacred Council likewise declares that it does not oppose efforts designed to introduce a perpetual calendar into civil society. But among the various systems which are being devised with a view to establishing a perpetual calendar and introducing it into civil life, those and only those are unopposed by the Church which retain and safeguard a seven-day week, with Sunday, without the introduction of any days outside the week, so that the succession of weeks may be left intact, unless in the judgment of the Apostolic See there are extremely weighty reasons to the contrary.

Sacram Liturgiam[1]

MOTU PROPRIO OF POPE PAUL VI

There is abundant evidence of the constant solicitude of Our predecessors and Ourselves, and of the bishops of the Church, for the preservation, the embellishment and – where needful – the reform of the sacred liturgy. Many, and well-known, published documents testify to it. A more recent indication is the Constitution on the Sacred Liturgy, which was approved, almost unanimously, by the Second Ecumenical Council of the Vatican, and which We had promulgated in solemn session on 4 December 1963.

The reason for such solicitude is that: 'in the earthly liturgy we take part in a foretaste of that heavenly liturgy which is celebrated in the holy city of Jerusalem, towards which we journey as pilgrims, where Christ is sitting at the right hand of God, a minister of the holies and of the true tabernacle; we sing a hymn to the Lord's glory with all the warriors of the heavenly army; venerating the memory of the saints, we hope for some part and fellowship with them; we eagerly await our Saviour, the Lord Jesus Christ, until he, our life, shall appear and we too will appear with him in glory' (Constitution on the Sacred Liturgy, no. 8).

And so it is that the faithful, when they thus worship God, the source and model of all holiness, are themselves drawn and, as it were, impelled to holiness; though still earth-bound pilgrims, they become 'contenders for the heavenly Sion, *almae Sionis aemuli*' (Lauds hymn, feast of the Dedication of a Church).

In the light of all this, it is easy to see why We so much want to see all Christians, and especially all priests, study the Constitution on the Liturgy and be prepared to put it wholeheartedly and loyally into execution as soon as it comes into force. In the nature of the case, there is need for the immediate implementation of the prescription bearing on the knowledge

1. The *Motu Proprio, Sacram Liturgiam*, was promulgated on 25 January 1964. A Latin text was published in the *Osservatore Romano* on 29 January 1964, and an Italian translation on 31 January. At the beginning of March the Vatican Polyglot Press published another Latin text – 'other' in the sense that there are a few, but important, differences between it and the earlier one. This second Latin text is, presumably, the official version. The translation which follows has been made from it. The text is annotated with lengthy excerpts from the authoritative commentary on the *Motu Proprio* by Father A. Bugnini, secretary of the post-conciliar liturgical commission. His commentary was published in the *Osservatore Romano* on 2–3 March 1964. The text of the *Motu Proprio* and the excerpts from Father Bugnini's commentary have been translated by Father Austin Flannery, O.P. (cf AAS, LVI, pp. 139-144).

and the promulgation of the liturgical laws. For this reason We appeal insistently to bishops of dioceses to set at once about teaching their people the power and the interior worth of the sacred liturgy, taking into account their age, condition in life and standard of religious culture, and using the help of their priests, 'the dispensers of the mysteries of Christ' (1 Cor. 4:1). Their shared knowledge will enable the faithful to take part in the religious services together, devoutly and with body and soul (Cf. Constitution, no. 19).

It is obvious, at the same time, that several prescriptions of the Constitution need time for their implementation: certain rites have to be revised and new editions of the liturgical books prepared. To ensure that this work will be carried out with the requisite wisdom and prudence, We have set up a special commission whose principal task it will be to see to the proper execution of the Constitution.

However, there are certain prescriptions of the Constitution which can be implemented at once. It is Our wish that these come into force without delay, so that the faithful will not be longer deprived of the spiritual benefits which are expected from them.

Therefore, with Our apostolic authority, and by means of this *Motu Proprio*, We order and decree that, from the coming first Sunday of Lent, which this year falls on 16 February, when the *vacatio legis* shall have been terminated, the following prescriptions shall come into force:

1. It is Our wish that seminaries, houses of study of religious orders, and faculties of theology set at once about incorporating into their curricula the prescriptions of Articles 15, 16 and 17 on the teaching of the liturgy, in such wise that they will be able to carry them out properly and diligently from the commencement of the next scholastic year.[2]

2. We decree, also, that, in accordance with the prescriptions of Articles 45 and 46, a commission be set up in every diocese whose task it will be, under the direction of the bishop, to promote the liturgy and understanding of the liturgy.

It would be advisable, also, that in some cases several dioceses should have a common commission.

Further, as far as possible, in every diocese two other commissions should be set up, one for sacred music and one for sacred art.

It will, in many cases, be convenient to unify those three diocesan commissions.

3. Further, it is Our wish that on the same date the prescription con-

---

2. Father Bugnini comments: 'Since there is question of ranking the liturgy amongst the "compulsory and major courses" . . . (Const., no. 16), and since this will entail re-arrangement of the number of hours and of years devoted to teaching . . ., it is clear that the congregation of seminaries and universities can be expected to issue directives as soon as possible so that the new arrangement can be put into execution properly (*ordinate*) and with the generous and intelligent co-operation and the goodwill (*diligenter*) of all those involved'.

tained in Article 52 – that there should be a homily during Mass on Sundays and holydays – should come into force.[3]

4. We also ordain that the portion of Article 71 which permits the conferring of the sacrament of confirmation during Mass, when opportunity offers, should become effective at once.[4]

5. With regard to Article 78: the sacrament of matrimony is normally to be administered during Mass, after the gospel and homily.[5]

We ordain that, whenever matrimony has to be administered outside of Mass, the following prescriptions are to be observed, until this rite will have been completely revised: after a brief address (see Constitution, Article 35, §3) the epistle and gospel from the nuptial Mass are to be read in the vernacular; then the nuptial blessing, which is contained in the Roman Ritual, tit. 8, ch. 3, is on every occasion (*semper*) to be imparted.[6]

6. Although the divine office has not yet been revised and reformed in

3. Father Bugnini remarks that this prescription (Number 3) merely reinforces article 52 of the Constitution, which is itself the echo of a centuries-old tradition; he refers to canon 1345 and number 747 of the new Code of Rubrics (1960). All this is evidence, he says, of the Church's will that 'the catechesis *within the Mass* should be a firm, immovable part of the pastoral ministry. No facile excuse can exempt the priest from the duty of addressing living words to the "holy assembly", expounding "what has been read", exhorting, enlightening and comforting, enlivening and nourishing the Christian life. At Mass the priest is the mouth-piece of God to the assembly of the faithful, he is the minister and the interpreter authorised by the Church'.

4. Father Bugnini comments: 'It is clear that there is question of the occasions when the number of those making their confirmation is not too great, and when pastoral reasons do not counsel otherwise'.

5. Father Bugnini comments: 'It would seem to be preferable that the rite should be administered by the priest who celebrates the Mass'.

6. Of the 'brief address', Father Bugnini says: 'This has the effect of erecting a first barrier against the profane, and of preparing the approach to a sacred action'. Noting that the blessing is to be given "on every occasion, *semper*", Father Bugnini remarks that therefore it is to be given whenever matrimony is celebrated during Lent and Advent, though this does not mean, he says, that licence is thereby given for the pomp and magnificence that would be out of keeping with the penitential character of these seasons. He goes on: 'The permission given for the administration of confirmation during Mass, and the clearly-expressed wish that matrimony be administered during Mass, are a re-statement of the principle that the Mass is the centre of worship; that it is from the altar that every grace and blessing descend on the faithful. For centuries the tradition was that it was during Mass, or in close connection with the Mass, that all the sacraments were administered, all the consecrations and the simple blessings – one thinks only of the blessing of the first-fruits at the *per quem haec omnia* of the Canon. All creatures were thus transformed and sanctified by the sacrifice of Christ.

'Students of pastoral liturgy have frequently remarked that certain sacramental rites, the most relevant and obligatory for the faithful, commence abruptly, dispensing with the necessary preparation of the spirit. But when they have been inserted into their native element, they take on greater significance'.

accordance with the prescriptions of Article 89, We grant to all those who are not obliged to the choral recitation of the office permission to omit the hour of Prime as from 16 February, and to choose amongst the remaining small hours the one that is most suitable to the time of day.

In making this concession, We are fully confident that sacred ministers will lose none of their piety as a result; rather, by performing their priestly duties diligently for the love of God, they will find themselves more intimately united to him all day long.[7]

7. Still with regard to the divine office, We ordain that the faculty can now be availed of by which ordinaries in individual cases and for a reasonable cause (*in casibus particularibus et de justa causa*) can dispense their subjects from the whole or from part of the obligation of reciting the divine office, or can exchange it for another obligation (see Constitution, Article 97).[8]

8. Still further with regard to the divine office, We wish to state that when members of the institutes of perfection recite, in obedience to their rules, some portion of the divine office, or some 'small office' based on the plan of the divine office and duly approved, they are to be considered as praying publicly with the Church (see Constitution, Article 98).

9. According to Article 101 of the Constitution, those who are obliged to the recitation of the divine office can be granted permission, in varying circumstances, to use a vernacular rendering instead of the Latin. We deem it opportune to specify that such vernacular renderings must be

7. Father Bugnini comments: 'The omission of Prime does not follow *ipso facto* from the Constitution, which merely foresees its suppression by the reform which is to be set in train, when its psalms and, perhaps, certain subsequent prayers will have been absorbed into other parts of the divine office. This is, therefore, a real and generous concession by the Holy Father.

'These two permissions are granted only to those who are not obliged to office in choir. In other words: all those who are obliged to the recitation of office in choir must continue to recite the whole of the divine office, just as they did up to 16 February. This holds good whether they are reciting it in common, or, for just reasons, have been dispensed from reciting it in choir and fulfil their obligation on their own. The matter is clearly stated in the Constitution, 95 (c).

'Here we touch on a perennial preoccupation of the Church. She has always regarded and always will regard public prayer as a great tribute of love to her divine Spouse. The Church's active life, in fact, is nourished and strengthened by the life of prayer. Canonical and religious communities are especially consecrated – by benefice, vocation, election – to prayer. It would be a grave loss to the mystical Spouse of Christ if this generous flood of prayer and petition were to abate. It is only for compelling reasons – such as pressing pastoral obligations – that the Church will lessen the obligation of the divine office. Indeed, at the same time she reminds the priest forcibly that his obligation of maintaining contact with God does not ease during the day'.

8. Describing this provision, Father Bugnini notes that while the *letter* qualifies the noun *causa* with the adjective, *justa*, the *spirit* would indicate the moral seriousness of the matter by adding the word 'exceptional' and 'only for particular cases'.

prepared and approved by the competent territorial ecclesiastical authority, in keeping with article 36, paragraphs 3 and 4, and that the 'acts' of this authority must be approved – that is to say, confirmed – by the Holy See, in keeping with article 36, paragraph 3.⁹ And we prescribe that this is always to be observed whenever a Latin liturgical text is translated into the vernacular by the aforesaid authority.¹⁰

10. According to Article 22, par. 2, the care of the liturgy is, within certain limits, vested in territorial episcopal conferences of various types. We lay down that the word 'territorial' is, for the time being, to be taken to mean 'national'.

As well as residential bishops, all those who are mentioned in Canon 292 of the Code of Canon Law can take part in these national conferences, with the right to vote. Further, coadjutor and auxiliary bishops can also be called to these conferences.

In these assemblies, a two-thirds majority by secret ballot is required for the making of legitimate decrees.

9. Since number nine, as it appeared in the first Latin version, occasioned considerable controversy, and since this controversy has now been set at rest by the present text, it may be useful to give the relevant portion in Latin: 'Quoniam vero ex Constit. art. 101, iis, qui divinum Officium recitare obstringuntur, aliter aliis facultas fit, pro latina, usurpandi linguam vernaculam, opportunum ducimus significare, varias huiusmodi populares interpretationes, a competente auctoritate ecclesiastica territoriali conficiendas et approbandas esse, ad normam art. 36, par. 3 et 4; acta vero huius auctoritatis, ad normam eiusdem art. 36, par. 3, ab Apostolica Sede esse rite probanda seu confirmanda'. Father Bugnini's Italian rendering of this last phrase is: 'devono essere approvati, vale a dire confermati, dalla Sede Apostolica'.

10. Father Bugnini comments: 'A question of great importance and of incalculable consequences. For four centuries, all power has been reserved to the Holy See in liturgical matters (can. 1257). The bishops' role was limited to seeing that the liturgical laws were observed and to overseeing popular devotions. The Constitution has broken down this centuries-old barrier. The Church is now in process of restoring to the competent "territorial" authorities – the word "territorial" is designedly elastic – many problems pertaining to the liturgy, including those of the introduction, the use and the limits to the use of the vernacular in certain rites.

'It is perfectly natural that the Holy See should be anxious that the change-over from the old discipline to the new should be effected prudently and gradually, and with such guarantees as the delicacy and the seriousness of the matter demand. For this reason the provision enshrined in number 9 cannot fail to meet with an intelligent understanding and to be a source of satisfaction to thoughtful people. . .

'The *Motu Proprio* accords full recognition to the competence of the various territorial authorities in the matter of vernacular renderings of liturgical texts, in keeping with paragraphs 3 and 4 of article 36. At the same time, it refers the "acts" of these authorities to the Holy See for confirmation. It is obvious that the word "acts" here covers the text of the vernacular rendering, and not merely the process by which the competent authority approved it'.

11. Lastly, We would draw attention to the fact that, apart from the innovations We have introduced by this apostolic letter, and apart from other changes whose implementation We have anticipated, the regulation of the sacred liturgy is vested exclusively in the Church: that is to say, in this apostolic See and, in the measure allowed by the law, in the bishop. For this reason, nobody else, not even a priest, is entitled to add, subtract or change anything in the liturgy (see Constitution, Article 22, 1 and 3).

We ordain that all that We have laid down in this *Motu Proprio* is to stand firm and is to be observed, no matter what else may stand contrary to it.

Given at Rome, in St Peter's, 25 January 1964, the feast of the Conversion of St Paul the Apostle, the first year of Our pontificate.[11]

11. Father Bugnini comments: 'At the end of his discourse at the promulgation of the Constitution, on 4 December 1963, the Holy Father warned that nobody was to meddle with "the official prayer of the Church, introducing private reforms or special rites", or to anticipate arbitrarily the implementation of the Constitution. It seems to me that the warning is addressed especially to the clergy. Any indiscretion, intemperate zeal or impulsiveness would harm and destroy the Constitution and the liturgy itself. It would be an irreparable crime, which would compromise the serious and calm labours of everybody else. It would not be constructive, but destructive, because the liturgy, "the Church's most noble prayer, ought to remain in harmonious concord throughout the world". It is clear, therefore, that whatever is not laid down in the *Motu Proprio*, even if it be in the Constitution, may not be effected by private initiative'.

Father Bugnini then spoke of the Pope's reference (at the promulgation of the Constitution) to the post-conciliar commissions. He went on: 'Thus, with a full sense of responsibility and with a large vision of the objectives to be attained, the liturgical Constitution is set on its journey. Its steps are cautious and prudent, but certain. They do not betray timidity or incertitude, but they reveal enlightened circumspection and a wise sense of balance, ensuring that the passage from the old to the new will be negotiated without loss of continuity, without sudden contrasts ... but by a gradual, natural evolution towards the perfect restoration of that wonderful masterpiece, the sacred liturgy'.

Instruction by the Sacred Congregation of Rites
on the

Proper Implementing
of the
Liturgy Constitution[1]

PREFACE

NATURE OF THIS INSTRUCTION

1. It is only fitting that the Constitution on Sacred Liturgy should be amongst the first fruits of the Second Ecumenical Council of the Vatican, since it regulates the Church's noblest activities. It will yield fruit more abundantly, the more profoundly pastors and the faithful are truly imbued with its spirit and the more willingly they implement it.

2. The *Consilium* for the implementation of the Constitution on Sacred Liturgy[2] – which Pope Paul VI established by the *Motu Proprio, Sacram Liturgiam* (25th January 1964) – has energetically set about the task confided to it : the faithful execution of the prescriptions of the Constitution and of the *Motu Proprio,* their interpretation and implementation.

3. It is of the greatest importance that, from the very beginning, these documents should be rightly implemented everywhere and that all possible doubts as to their interpretation should be eliminated. It is for this reason that the *Consilium,* on the instructions

1. The following translation was made by Father Austin Flannery, O.P., from the Latin text which was published in the *Osservatore Romano,* 18 October, 1964. The headings were in the original, the footnotes were added by the translator.

2. *Consilium ad exequendam Constitutionem de Sacra Liturgia,* under the presidency of Cardinal Lercaro. The *'Consilium,'* which prepared this document is quite distinct from the Congregation of Rites, which issued it. See *Doctrine and Life,* May, 1964, pp. 321-323. Throughout this translation we have retained the Latin word *Consilium* for this post-conciliar commission. The Italian translation in the *Osservatore Romano* does the same.

of the Holy Father, has prepared the present Instruction. It defines more clearly the competence of episcopal conferences in liturgical matters, it makes more specific what was expressed in general terms in both documents, it permits, or decrees, certain changes which can be introduced prior to the revision of the liturgical books.

PRINCIPLES TO BE BORNE IN MIND

4. The practical directives which now follow have for their object to make the liturgy correspond more perfectly with the mind of the Council – to promote, that is to say, the active participation of the faithful. Further, the general reform of the liturgy will be better received by the faithful if it is accomplished gradually, and if it is proposed and explained to them properly by their pastors.

5. First of all, however, it is essential that everybody be persuaded that the scope of the Constitution on the Sacred Liturgy is not limited merely to the changing of liturgical rites and texts. Rather is it its aim to foster the formation of the faithful and that pastoral activity of which the liturgy is the summit and source (see Const., Art. 10). The changes in the liturgy which have already been introduced, or which will be introduced later, have this same end in view.

6. Pastoral activity which is centred on the liturgy aims to make the Paschal Mystery be expressed in men's lives.[3] It was in the Paschal Mystery that the Son of God incarnate, having been obedient unto the death of the cross, was raised so high by his resurrection and ascension that he was able to share his own divine life with the world, in such wise that men who had been dead to sin and were now made like to Christ 'may not now live to themselves, but unto him who died for them, and rose again' (2 Cor. 5 :15).

This is accomplished by faith and by the sacraments of faith -- especially, that is to say, by baptism (see Const., Art. 6), by the sacred mystery of the Eucharist, the pivot of all the other sacraments and sacramentals (see Const., Art. 47), and also by the cycle of celebrations in which, throughout the Church's year, the paschal mystery of Christ is unfolded (see Const., Art. 102-107).

7. Consequently, even though the liturgy is not the whole of the Church's activity (see Const., Art. 9), great care must be taken

---

3. The Latin of this sentence is: *Vis autem huius actionis pastoralis circa Liturgiam ordinandae in eo posita est ut Mysterium paschale vivendo exprimatur.* The Italian translation published in the *Osservatore Romano* reads as follows: *Lo sforzo di questa azione pastorale incentrata nella liturgia deve tendere a far vivere il mistero pasquale.*

that pastoral work be properly linked with it (*ut opera pastoralia cum sacra liturgia debite connectantur*). At the same time, the liturgical apostolate must not be exercised separately and, as it were, in a vacuum. It should be closely linked with other pastoral activities.

It is especially necessary that there be close links between liturgy, catechesis, religious instruction and preaching.

8. Bishops and their helpers in the priesthood, therefore, should set great store by their whole liturgy-centred apostolate. Thus the faithful too, by perfect participation in the liturgy will receive the divine life abundantly and, having become Christ's leaven and the salt of the earth, they will announce and transmit it to others.

CHAPTER ONE:

CERTAIN GENERAL NORMS

HOW THESE NORMS WILL APPLY

9. The practical norms contained in the Constitution and in this Instruction as well as the changes which, even prior to the reform of the liturgical books, are by this same Instruction permitted or decreed, all apply solely to the Roman rite. However, they may be adopted by the other Latin rites, due allowance being made for the demands of the law.

10. Whatever measures this Instruction submits to the jurisdiction of the competent territorial ecclesiastical authority, it is this same authority, alone, which can and must put them into effect, by legitimate decrees.

In every case, the time and circumstances in which decrees become binding must be indicated. A sufficient interval of time should be allowed for notification of the faithful and for instructing them in the observance of the decrees.

LITURGICAL FORMATION OF THE CLERGY
(Const., Art. 15, 16, 18)

11. With regard to the liturgical formation of the clergy :
   (a) Theological faculties are to have a chair of liturgy, so that all students may be properly instructed in the liturgy; local ordinaries and major religious superiors should see to the provision, as soon as possible, of properly trained professors of liturgy in seminaries and in studentates for religious;
   (b) Professors who are given charge of courses in sacred liturgy

must be trained, as soon as possible, in accordance with Article 15 of the Constitution.[4]

(c) Where possible, institutes of pastoral liturgy must be set up for further training of the clergy, especially of those who are already engaged in the apostolate.

12. Liturgy courses must be of appropriate duration, to be decided by the responsible authority, and must follow a proper method, in accordance with Article 15 of the Constitution.

   13. Liturgical ceremonies should be celebrated with the utmost perfection. For this reason :

(a) The rubrics are to be observed carefully and the ceremonies to be performed with dignity, under the watchful scrutiny of the ecclesiastical superiors. They should be practised beforehand.

(b) Each cleric should frequently exercise the liturgical activities proper to his order; the activities, that is to say, of deacon, subdeacon, acolyte, reader and, further, commentator and chanter.

(c) Churches and oratories, church furnishings and vestments should be examples of genuine, modern Christian art.[5]

LITURGICAL FORMATION OF THE SPIRITUAL LIFE OF THE CLERGY (Const., Art. 17)

14. In seminaries and in studentates for religious the Constitution on Sacred Liturgy must be fully implemented, in accordance with the directives of the Holy See, and through the combined efforts of superiors and teachers; this to the end that the clerical students be taught to take part fully in the liturgical ceremonies and to draw from them nourishment both for their own spiritual lives and for communication to others later. They should be properly initiated

4. Art 15 of the Constitution directs that they should be trained in institutes which specialise in this subject : *in institutis ad hoc speciali cura destinatis probe instituendi sunt*. As was noted in *Doctrine and Life,* February, 1964 (p. 136, footnote 36). 'The institutes which are of pontifical rank, and can confer degrees, are the *Pontificium Institutum Liturgicum,* Sant' Anselmo, Rome, Italy and *L'Institut Supérieur de Liturgie de Paris,* France. The institute at Trier, Germany (*Nova Sedes Instituti Liturgici Trevirensis*) has up to now been primarily for research.' See *Ephemerides Liturgicae,* 1962, pp. 53-57.

5. It is perhaps arguable that the translation does not fully convey the meaning of the Latin original at this point; that the text does not opt exclusively for contemporary art, but merely grants it right of entry. The original is as follows : *ecclesiae et oratoria, sacra suppellex in genere et sacrae vestes speciem genuinae artis christianae, etiam hodiernae, praeseferant.* The translator put the problem to the officials of the *Consilium* and was told that the meaning is that contemporary art *must* be used.

into the liturgy, by the following means : by recommending to them, and by stocking their libraries with, a sufficient quantity of books which treat of the liturgy under its theological and spiritual aspects especially; by means of meditations and sermons drawn primarily from sacred scripture and from the liturgy (see Const., Art. 35, par. 2); by the communal practice of all the traditional customs of the Christian life, in conformity with the liturgical seasons.

15. The daily celebration of the Eucharist, which is the centre of the spiritual life, should take the form best adapted to the condition of the participants (see Const., Art. 19).

On Sundays and on the greater feasts there should be Mass *in cantu* and all those who are at home should take part. There should be a homily and, as far as possible, those who are not priests should receive Holy Communion. Priests who are not needed for individual Masses for the faithful may concelebrate, especially on the more solemn feasts, after the new rite will have been published.

It is desirable (*expedit*) that seminarians should take part in the Eucharistic celebration with the bishop in the cathedral, at least on the great feasts (see Const., Art. 41).

16. It is very desirable that clerical students who are not yet bound to the divine office should recite or sing Lauds in common daily as morning prayer and Vespers as evening prayer, or Compline at the end of the day. As far as possible, the professors themselves should take part in this common exercise. Further, clerics who are in sacred orders should be given sufficient time for the recitation of the divine office through the day.

It is very desirable that, when possible, seminarians should sing Vespers in the cathedral, at least on the great feasts.

17. Pious practices which owe their origin to the customs or the laws of a locality or institute should be accorded due reverence. Care should be taken, however, especially if they are performed in common, that they be in keeping with the liturgy, in accordance with Article 13 of the Constitution, and that they take account of the liturgical seasons.

THE LITURGICAL FORMATION OF RELIGIOUS

18. What has been said in the foregoing articles about the spiritual formation of the clergy must be applied to members of the 'states of perfection,' both men and women.

LITURGICAL FORMATION OF THE FAITHFUL
(Const., Art. 19)

19. Pastors of souls are to make it their business (*annitantur*) to implement, with care and patience, the precepts of the Constitution

on the instruction of the faithful in the liturgy, and on their active participation in it, internally and externally, 'taking into account their age and condition, their way of life and standard of religious culture' (Const., Art. 19). They should take special care that members of religious associations for layfolk be instructed in the liturgy and take an active part in it. It is the role of such associations to share more intimately in the life of the Church and to assist pastors in organizing the liturgical life of the parish (see Const., Art. 42).

THE COMPETENT AUTHORITY IN LITURGICAL MATTERS (Const., Art. 22)

20. It belongs to the Church's authority to regulate the sacred liturgy. Nobody, therefore, is allowed to proceed on his own initiative in this domain, for this would be to the detriment of the liturgy itself, more often than not, and of the reform which the competent authority has to carry out.

21. It is for the Holy See to reform and to approve liturgical books for general use, to regulate the sacred liturgy for the universal Church, to approve or confirm the 'Acts' and deliberations of the territorial authorities and to receive the proposals or petitions of these same territorial authorities.

22. It is for the bishop to regulate the liturgy in his own diocese, in accordance with the norms and the spirit of the Constitution on Sacred Liturgy, the decrees of the Holy See and of the competent territorial authority.

23. *For the time being* (*interim*) the various types of territorial conferences (*coetus*) of bishops which are invested with authority to regulate the liturgy, according to Article 22, 2, of the Constitution, are to be understood to be the following :

   (a) either the conference of all the bishops of one nation, in accordance with the *Motu Proprio, Sacram Liturgiam*, number 10;[6]

   (b) or a conference, already legitimately constituted, embracing the bishops, or the bishops and other local ordinaries, of several nations;

   (c) or a conference yet to be constituted, with the consent of the Holy See, of bishops, or of bishops and other local ordinaries, of several nations. Such a solution is envisaged especially where the bishops in each nation are so few that it would be better for the bishops of nations which share the

---

6. The *Motu Proprio* states : ' We lay down that the word " *territorial* " is, for the time being, to be taken to mean " national."

same language and the same civil culture to form one conference.

If, however, a particular local situation seems to demand a different solution, the matter should be referred to the Holy See.

24. The following must be invited to such conferences :
(a) Residential bishops;
(b) Abbots and prelates *nullius;*
(c) Vicars and Prefects Apostolic;
(d) Apostolic administrators of dioceses who have been permanently appointed;
(e) all other local ordinaries, with the exception of Vicars General.

Co-adjutor and auxiliary bishops may be invited to attend by the president, with the consent of the majority of those present who have deliberative votes.

25. Unless special local conditions legitimately demand another solution, a conference is to be called together :
(a) by its respective president, when there is question of a conference already legitimately constituted;
(b) otherwise, by the archbishop or the bishop who has the legal right of precedence.

26. The president, with the consent of the Fathers, is to decide the order of the business to be transacted, he opens the meeting, transfers it, prorogues and closes it.

27. All those mentioned in number 24 have deliberative votes, not excluding co-adjutor and auxiliary bishops, unless the document by which the meeting is convened expressly states otherwise.

28. For the legitimate enactment of decrees, a two-thirds majority, by secret vote, is required.

29. When the 'Acts' of a territorial conference of bishops are being sent to the Holy See for approval, or confirmation, they should contain the following :
(a) the names of those who were present at the conference,
(b) an account of the proceedings,
(c) the results of the voting on each decree.

Two copies of the 'Acts,' signed by the president and secretary of the conference, and properly sealed, must be sent to the *Consilium* for the Implementation of the Constitution on Sacred Liturgy.

30. In accordance with the Constitution, Article 36, par. 3, and with the *Motu Proprio, Sacram Liturgiam,* number 9, when there is question of 'Acts' which contain decrees on the introduction of the vernacular into the liturgy, and on the extent to which it is to be used, the following details, in addition to those listed in the preceeding number, must be attended to :

(a) all the portions of the liturgy which it has been decided to say in the vernacular must be indicated;

(b) two copies of the liturgical texts in the vernacular must be furnished, one of which will be restored to the conference;

(c) a short description of the criteria on which the translation is based must be appended.

31. The decrees of the territorial conferences which need the approval, or confirmation, of the Holy See must not be promulgated or implemented until they have received it.

DIVISION OF LITURGICAL FUNCTIONS TO BE OBSERVED (Const., Art. 28)

32. If the parts which belong to the choir and the people are chanted or recited by them, they must not be said privately by the celebrant.

33. Similarly, the celebrant must not say privately the readings which are read or sung by the competent minister or the altar-server.

NOT RESPECTING PERSONS (Const., Art. 32)

34. Bishops – or, if it seems opportune, regional or national episcopal conferences – are to see to the implementation, in their territories, of the prescription of the holy Council which forbids the according of special honours, either in ceremonies or by external display, to private persons or to social classes.

35. For the rest, in liturgical ceremonies, and especially in the celebration of Mass and in the administration of the sacraments and of the sacramentals, pastors should, with prudence and charity, see to it that the equality of all the faithful is expressed, even externally, and that any appearance of money-making is avoided (*ut . . . omnis species quaestus vitetur*).

THE SIMPLIFICATION OF CERTAIN RITES (Const., Art. 34)

36. In order that liturgical ceremonies may have that noble simplicity which is in keeping with the mind of our age :

(a) obeisances (*inclinationes*) by celebrants and ministers to the choir will be made only at the beginning and the end of sacred ceremonies;

(b) incensation of the clergy, apart from those who are

bishops, is to be made collectively, by a triple incensation to each part of the choir;

(c) only the altar at which the liturgical ceremony takes place is to be incensed;

(d) the kissing of hands and of objects given or received is to be omitted.

BIBLE SERVICES (Const., Art. 35, par 4)

37. Where there is a shortage of priests, if there is no priest to celebrate Mass on a Sunday or Holy Day of obligation, a Bible service is recommended, subject to the judgment of the local ordinary, under the presidency of a deacon or a layman deputed for the task.

The structure of this Bible service is to be the same as that of the liturgy of the Word at Mass : the Epistle and Gospel of the day's Mass are generally read in the vernacular; chants, especially from the psalms, being sung at the beginning of the service and during it. The person who presides should preach, if he is a deacon; if he is not a deacon, he should read a homily chosen by the bishop or the parish priest. The service should terminate with 'the community prayer,' or 'the prayer of the faithful,' and the Lord's prayer.

38. It is fitting that Bible services on the vigils of great feasts, on certain ferial days of Lent and Advent, on Sundays and feastdays, should also have the same structure as the liturgy of the Word at Mass, though it is quite permissible to have only one reading.

If there is more than one reading, however, the reading from the Old Testament normally precedes the reading from the New Testament, and the reading of the Gospel is the culmination of the service; when this is done, the sequence of salvation history is perceived more clearly.

39. In order that these services be performed with dignity and reverence, the diocesan liturgical commissions will give whatever assistance is needed.

VERNACULAR RENDERINGS OF THE LITURGICAL TEXTS (Const., Art. 36, par. 3)

40. When, in accordance with Article 36, par. 3, of the Constitution, liturgical texts are being translated into the vernacular, it is well to observe the following directives :

(a) The translations of the liturgical texts are to be made from the Latin liturgical text. The version used for the Biblical pericopes must conform to the Latin text used in the liturgy, though it is permissable to correct this in the light of the original text or of a more faithful version.

(b) The preparation of the vernacular rendering should, preferably, be entrusted to the liturgical commission – described in Article 44 of the Constitution and in number 44 of this Instruction – with the help, if possible, of the Institute of pastoral liturgy. Where such a commission does not exist, the preparation of the vernacular liturgy should be entrusted to two or three bishops, who will seek the help of experts – not excluding lay people – in Sacred Scripture, liturgy, biblical languages, Latin, the vernacular language and music. A perfect translation, in fact, must needs fulfil several conditions.

(c) When occasion demands, bishops of neighbouring countries of the same language should take counsel together.

(d) In countries where there is more than one language, there should be a translation for each language and it should be examined carefully by the bishops concerned.

(e) Care must be taken for the dignity of the books from which the liturgical texts are read to the people in the vernacular; in such wise that the very appearance of the book will excite the faithful to greater reverence for the word of God and of sacred things.

41. Wherever there is a group of people who share a language other than that of the region in which they find themselves – as happens especially with emigrants, in 'personal' parishes and such like – it is permissible to use the language they know, in liturgical ceremonies, provided one has the consent of the local ordinary and provided the version used has been legitimately approved by the competent territorial ecclesiastical authority for that language.

42. New melodies, for the parts of the vernacular liturgy which have to be chanted by the celebrant and ministers, must be approved by the competent territorial ecclesiastical authority.

43. Particular liturgical books, which were legitimately approved prior to the promulgation of the Constitution on the Sacred Liturgy, remain in force, as do concessions granted up to that date, provided they are not contrary to the Constitution and until such time as, the liturgical reform having been completed wholly or in part, it shall be decreed otherwise.

REGIONAL LITURGICAL COMMISSIONS
(Const., Art. 44)

44. When a territorial authority sets up a liturgical commission, it must be drawn from the ranks of the bishops themselves, as far as possible; alternatively, it may comprise one or more bishops, with the addition of priests who are expert in liturgy and pastoral

matters, and who have been selected by name for this office.

It is fitting that the members of this commission, and its consultors, should meet several times a year, for discussion.

45. The territorial authority may fittingly entrust the following matters to such a commission :

(a) The promotion of investigations and experiments, in accordance with Article 40, pars 1 and 2, of the Constitution.

(b) The promotion of practical initiatives in the territory as a whole, for fostering the liturgy and the implementation of the Constitution on sacred liturgy.

(c) The preparation of the investigations and the assistance needed for the implementation of the decrees of the plenary assembly of bishops.

(d) The direction of the pastoral liturgical programme of the region as a whole, the superintendence of the implementation of the decrees of the assembly of bishops, and reporting on this to the assembly.

(e) The promotion of frequent contacts with groups in the same territory which are concerned with the Bible, catechetics, pastoral matters, music, sacred art. They should foster similar contacts with every manner of pious associations of the laity. They should also promote initiatives in common with all these groups.

46. The members of the institute of pastoral liturgy, and the experts who are selected to assist the liturgical commission, must not refuse requests by individual bishops for assistance in the more effective promotion of the liturgical apostolate in their own territories.

THE DIOCESAN LITURGICAL COMMISSION
(Const., Art. 45)

47. The diocesan liturgical commission, under the guidance of the bishop :

(a) must acquaint themselves with the state of pastoral liturgical activity in the diocese;

(b) must diligently implement what has been proposed by the competent authority, at the same time acquainting themselves with investigations and initiatives which have been undertaken elsewhere in the same field;

(d) in individual cases, or even for the diocese as a whole, they must suggest opportune plans for the progress of pastoral liturgical action; they must indicate, and even select, suitable people who can, as occasion offers, assist the clergy in this matter; they must propose whatever material helps they deem necessary (*apta instrumenta atque subsidia proponere*);

(c) they must suggest and promote practical initiatives which can contribute to the progress of the liturgy, with an eye to assisting, especially, the priests who are already engaged in the apostolate;

(e) they must see to it that, in the diocese, all initiatives directed towards the promotion of the liturgy are in mutual accord and that the different groups help one another, in a manner analogous to what was described for the liturgical commission attached to the assembly of bishops (number 45 [e]).

CHAPTER TWO:

THE EUCHARISTIC MYSTERY

THE ORDER OF THE MASS (Const., Art. 50)

48.   Until the entire Order of the Mass will have been reformed, the following directives are to be observed :

(a) The portions of the Proper which are sung or recited by the choir or by the people are not to be said privately by the celebrant.

(b) The portions of the Ordinary may be sung or recited with the choir or people by the celebrant.

(c) In the prayers said at the foot of the altar at the beginning of Mass, Psalm 42 is to be omitted. All the prayers at the foot of the altar are to be omitted whenever another liturgical function immediately precedes the celebration of Mass.

(d) In a solemn Mass, the paten is not held by the subdeacon, but is left on the altar.

(e) The Secret, or 'prayer over the offerings,' is to be chanted at Masses in cantu[7] and in other Masses is to be said aloud.

(f) The doxology at the end of the Canon of the Mass, from the words *Per ipsum* to *Per omnia saecula saeculorum,* and the response *Amen,* inclusively, are to be chanted or said aloud.

---

7. The Instruction uses the terms, *Missa solemnis, Missa in cantu* and *Missa cantata.* It seems obvious that these are to understood in the sense given to them by the *Instruction on Sacred Music and Liturgy,* of 1958. The term, *Missa in cantu,* 'Mass with singing,' therefore, is a generic term embracing both Solemn Mass (High Mass, with priest, deacon and subdeacon) and the *Missa Cantata,* or sung Mass (priest and servers). To avoid confusion, we have used the term 'Mass *in cantu*' for this generic sense, using 'Sung Mass' to translate *Missa cantata.* See H. A. REINHOLD, *Bringing the Mass to the People,* Burns and Oates, London 1960, p. 39. Father Reinhold's book will be found very useful for an understanding of the liturgical reasoning behind the present chapter of the Instruction.

During the whole of the doxology the celebrant is to hold the chalice and the host slightly elevated, he is to omit the signs of the cross and, at the end, he is to genuflect only after the people have answered *Amen.*

(g) The ' Our Father' can be said in the vernacular by the people and celebrant at said Masses; at Masses *in cantu,* however, celebrant and people may sing it together in Latin or, if the territorial ecclesiastical authority so decree, in the vernacular, using a melody approved by the same authority.

(h) The embolism[8] which follows the Our Father, is to be chanted or said aloud.

(i) The formula *Corpus Christi* is to be used in the distribution of Holy Communion. As he says the words, the celebrant is to hold the host, slightly elevated, over the ciborium, showing it to the communicant, who is to reply, *Amen.* The celebrant then gives him Holy Communion, omitting the sign of the cross with the host.

(j) The last gospel is to be omitted; the Leonine prayers are suppressed.[9]

(k) It is permissible to celebrate Mass *in cantu,* with a deacon only.[10]

(l) When necessary, bishops may celebrate Mass *in cantu* after the manner of priests.

THE READINGS AND THE INTERVENING CHANTS
(Const., Art. 51)

49. In public Masses, the Lessons,[11] the Epistle and the Gospel, are to be read or sung facing the people :

8. i.e. the prayer, *Libera nos.*

9. 'The Last Gospel was not regarded as a part of the Mass during the Middle Ages. It was first used by the Dominicans. Besides being anticlimatic after the Service of the Word, it has the additional disadvantage of being inaudible at High Mass.' Reinhold, op. cit., p. 74. The Leonine prayers were never intended to be a permanent part of the Mass; for some time past they have been said for the conversion of Russia.

10. Permission to celebrate solemn Mass without the assistance of a subdeacon, the *Missa cum diacono,* has been fairly widely granted hitherto. It has been permitted throughout the Roman rite during Holy Week since 1957; see S.C.R. *ordinationes et declarationes* (Feb. 1, 1957) A.A.S. 49, 91-95. See Reinhold, op. cit., p. 18.

11. Article 51 of the Constitution says that 'the treasures of the Bible are to be opened up more lavishly,' and liturgical scholars have for some time been recommending that readings from the Old Testament be a normal prelude to the reading of the Epistle. (See Reinhold, op. cit., p. 52). Presumably, the ' Lessons ' (*Lectiones*) referred to here are those from the Old Testament. (Throughout this translation, we have used the word 'readings' to translate the generic term, *'lectiones'* (with small 'l')

(a) at a solemn Mass, from an ambo or at the altar-rails;

(b) at a sung Mass and at a said Mass, if it is the celebrant who is reading or chanting them, he may do so from the altar, from the ambo, or from the altar-rails, whichever is the more suitable; if anybody else is reading or singing them, however, he must do so from the ambo or the altar-rails.

50. In non-solemn, public Masses,[12] the Lessons and the Epistle, together with the intervening chants, can be read by a suitable reader or altar-server, the celebrant being seated and listening; the Gospel, however, can be read by a deacon or a priest, who is to say *Munda cor meum,* ask for a blessing and, at the end, offer the book of the Gospels to the celebrant to be kissed.

51. In Masses *in cantu,* if the vernacular is used for the Lessons, the Epistle and Gospel, they may be read, the chanting of them being dispensed with.

52. When the Lessons, the Epistle, the intervening chants and the Gospel are being read or sung, the following procedure is to be observed :

(a) In a solemn Mass, the celebrant, seated, listens to the Lessons, the Epistle and the intervening chants. When the Epistle has been sung or read, the subdeacon goes to the celebrant and is blessed by him. Then the celebrant, seated, puts incense into the thurible and blesses it. While the *Alleluia* and verse is being sung – or towards the end of whatever other chants follow the Epistle – the celebrant rises and blesses the deacon; standing at the seat, he listens to the Gospel, kisses the Gospel-book and, after the homily, intones the Creed, if it is to be sung. After the Creed has been finished, he returns to the altar with his ministers, unless he has to direct the 'prayer of the faithful.'

(b) In sung Masses or said Masses in which the Lessons, the Epistle, the chants which follow the Epistle, and the Gospel, are chanted or read by a minister, as outlined in number 50, the celebrant should follow the directives given above.

(c) In sung Masses and said Masses in which he himself reads or chants the Gospel in an ambo or at the altar-rails, the celebrant goes over to the altar while the *Alleluia* and verse is being sung – or towards the end of whatever chants

---

12. It could be argued that the rendering 'public Masses' for *Missae cum populo celebratae* ('Masses celebrated with the people') fails to communicate the Instruction's reluctance to adopt a formula which seems to ignore the Constitution's assertion that 'every Mass has of itself a public and social nature' (Art. 27). However, the formula 'public Mass,' in its normal English usage, does seem to convey the Instruction's meaning adequately.

follow the Epistle – and, bowing in front of the lowest altar step, he says *Munda cor meum* and then goes to the ambo or the altar-rails to sing or read the Gospel.

(d) If, however, during a sung Mass or a said Mass the celebrant himself sings or reads all the readings in the ambo or at the altar-rails, he must read the intervening chants in the same place. He says *Munda cor meum*, however, facing the altar.

THE HOMILY (Const., Art. 52)

53. There must be a homily at every public Mass on Sundays and holy days of obligation. No exception is made for sung conventual Mass or for pontifical Mass. Apart from holy days, it is recommended that there be a homily on certain ferial days during Advent and Lent, and on other occasions when the faithful go to church in larger numbers.

54. The 'homily from the sacred text' is to be understood to be either an explanation of certain aspects of the readings from Sacred Scripture, or of some other text from the Ordinary or the Proper of the day, taking into account, however, the mystery which is being celebrated and the peculiar needs of the congregation.

55. If a scheme for preaching is drawn up for certain times of the year, it should be closely and harmoniously linked with – at least – the principal seasons and feasts of the liturgical year (see Const., Art 102-104). It should be linked, that is to say, with the mystery of the Redemption. The homily is part of the liturgy of the day.

THE PRAYER OF THE FAITHFUL (Const., Art. 53)

56. Where the 'community prayer,' or the 'prayer of the faithful,'[13] has already become customary, it should be said before the Offertory and after the *Oremus*, using the formulae existing in each region, for the time being. The celebrant is to direct the prayer from the celebrant's seat, or from the altar, the ambo or the altar-rails.

The intentions or invocations can be sung by a deacon, a chanter, or by some other suitable server. The celebrant, however,

---

13. Father Reinhold gives a sample, composed by Father Balthasar Fischer, in his *Bringing the Mass to the People*, pp. 56-57. Another sample is contained in the Good Friday liturgy. See also *L'Eglise en Prière*, by G. MARTIMORT, Paris 1962, pp. 358-360.

is to say the words of introduction and the concluding prayer, which, normally, will be the prayer 'God our refuge and our strength' (see *Missale Romanum, Orationes diversae*, No. 20). An alternative prayer which answers better to a particular need may be substituted for it, however.

Where, however, the 'community prayer,' or 'prayer of the faithful,' is not customary, the competent territorial ecclesiastical authority can order it to be done, along the lines indicated above, using, for the time being, formulae approved by itself.

WHERE THE VERNACULAR MAY BE USED IN THE MASS (Const., Art. 54)

57. The competent territorial ecclesiastical authority, its 'Acts' being subject to the approval or confirmation of the Holy See, can allow the vernacular in public Masses, whether *in cantu* or said, as follows :

(a) for the Lessons, the Epistle and Gospel, and in the 'prayer of the faithful,' especially;

(b) as local conditions suggest, in the chants of the Ordinary of the Mass – in the *Kyrie, Gloria, Credo, Sanctus-Benedictus* and *Agnus Dei* – in the Introit, Offertory and Communion antiphons, and in the chants between the readings;

(c) further, in the acclamations, the salutations and the dialogue formulae, in the formulae : *Ecce Agnus Dei, Domine non sum dignus* and *Corpus Christi* in the communion of the faithful, and in the Lord's Prayer, the introductory admonition to it, and its embolism.

Missals for liturgical use, however, must have the Latin text as well as the vernacular text.

58. Only the Holy See can grant permission for the vernacular in the other parts of the Mass which are said by the celebrant alone.

59. Pastors of souls should take care that the faithful, and especially those who are members of pious associations of layfolk, are also able to recite or sing in Latin – at any rate, in the simpler melodies – the portions of the Ordinary of the Mass which pertain to them.

REPEATING HOLY COMMUNION ON THE SAME DAY (Const., Art. 55)

60. The faithful who have received Holy Communion during the Mass of the Easter Vigil, or during the Mass of the night of the Lord's Nativity, may receive Holy Communion again at the second Paschal Mass and at one of the Masses of Christmas Day.

CHAPTER THREE:

THE OTHER SACRAMENTS

AND THE SACRAMENTALS

THE EXTENSION OF THE VERNACULAR
(Const., Art. 63)

61. The competent territorial ecclesiastical authority, its 'Acts' being subject to approval or confirmation by the Holy See, can allow the vernacular:
> (a) in the rites of Baptism, Confirmation, Penance, the Anointing of the Sick – the essential formula by no means being excepted – and in the distribution of Holy Communion;
> (b) in the administration of Holy Orders: in the allocutions given at the beggining of every Ordination or Consecration, in the examination of the bishop-elect in an episcopal Consecration, and in the admonitions;
> (c) in sacramentals;
> (d) at funerals.

If a wider use of the vernacular seems desirable in any locality, the prescription of Art. 40 of the Constitution, should be observed.

SUPPLYING FOR OMISSIONS IN BAPTISM
(Const., Art. 69)

62. In the Order for supplying for ommissions in the Baptism[14] of an infant, as it is outlined in the Roman Ritual, tit. II, c.5, the following exorcisms are to be omitted: number 66 (*Exi ab eo*), number 10 (*Exorcizo te, immunde spiritus; Ergo maledicte diabole*), number 15 (*Exorcizo te, omnis spiritus*).

63. In the Order for supplying for omissions in the Baptism of an adult, as it is found in the Roman Ritual, tit. II, c.6, the following exorcisms are to be omitted: number 5 (*Exi ab eo*), number 15 (*Ergo, maledicte diabole*), number 17 (*Audi maledicte satana*), number 19 (*Exorcizo te . . . Ergo maledicte diabole*), number 21 (*Ergo, maledicte diabole*), number 23 (*Ergo, maledicte diabole*), number 25 (*Exorcizo te . . . Ergo, maledicte diabole*), number 31 (*Non te latet*) and number 33 (*Exi, immunde spiritus*).

---

14. This section refers to Baptisms performed in danger of death, and using only the minimum essential formula. If the person lives, the rites ommitted must be supplied later, in a subsequent ceremony.

CONFIRMATION   (Const., Art. 71)

64. If Confirmation is administered during Mass, it is fitting that the Mass be celebrated by the bishop himself, who should, in that case, administer Confirmation in his Mass vestments.

The Mass during which Confirmation is administered can be a votive Mass, second class, of the Holy Spirit.

65. After the Gospel and the homily, it is fitting that those who are to be confirmed should renew their baptismal vows, according to the legitimate custom of each region, unless they have already done this before Mass.

66. If the Mass is celebrated by somebody other than the bishop, it is fitting that he should assist at the Mass, wearing the vestments prescribed for the administration of confirmation. These can be the same colour as the Mass-vestments, or they can be white. The bishop should preach the homily, and the celebrant should not resume the Mass until Confirmation has been administered.

67. Confirmation must be administered according to the rite described in the Roman Pontifical, but only one sign of the cross should be made at the words, *In nomine Patris et Filii et Spiritus Sancti*, which follow the formula, *Signo te*.

THE ANOINTING OF THE SICK AND VIATICUM
(Const., Art. 74)

68. When the Anointing of the Sick and Viaticum are administered together, unless a particular Ritual already has a continuous rite,[15] the matter is to be arranged as follows : after the sprinkling of holy water and the entrance prayer of the rite of Anointing, the priest hears the confession of the sick person, if this be necessary. He then administers the Anointing and, lastly, Viaticum, omitting the sprinkling and its formulae, the confiteor and the absolution.

If, however, the apostolic blessing and plenary indulgence at the hour of death is to be administered, this is to be done immediately before the Anointing, omitting the sprinkling and its formulae, the confiteor and the absolution.

THE IMPOSITION OF HANDS AT THE
CONSECRATION OF A BISHOP   (Const., Art. 76)

69. At the Consecration of a bishop, all the bishops present, wearing choral dress, can take part in the imposition of hands.

---

15. Many National Rituals, including The Irish Ritual, already have a 'continuous rite' : *rituus continuus*.

Only the consecrating bishop and the two co-consecrating bishops, however, can pronounce the words : *Accipe Spiritum Sanctum.*

THE RITE OF MATRIMONY (Const., Art. 78)

70. Matrimony, unless there is a just cause for omitting Mass, should be celebrated during Mass, after the Gospel and the homily, which latter should never be omitted.

71. Whenever Matrimony is celebrated during Mass, the Mass should – in keeping with the rubrics and even during the forbidden times[16] – be the votive Mass for the bride and groom, or should have a commemoration of it.

72. As far as possible, the parish priest himself – or his delegate – who assists at the marriage, should also celebrate the Mass. If, however, the priest who assists at the marriage is not the celebrant of the Mass, the celebrant may not go on with the Mass before the marriage rite has been completed.

If a priest merely assists at the marriage, and does not celebrate the Mass, he should wear a surplice and white stole and, if such is the local custom, a cope, and he should preach the homily. It is the priest who celebrates the Mass, however, who should impart the blessing between the *Pater Noster* and the *Placet.*

73. The nuptial blessing is always to be given during Mass, even during the forbidden times, and even if one or both of the partners has been married before.

74. In the celebration of Matrimony outside of Mass, the following directives are to be observed :

(a) At the beginning of the ceremony, in accordance with the *Motu Proprio, Sacram Liturgiam,* number 5, a short 'admonition' should be given. It is not to be a homily, but a simple introduction to the ceremony (see Const., Art. 35, 3). A sermon, or homily, from the sacred text (see Const., Art. 52), must be given after the reading of the Epistle and Gospel of the Mass for the bride and groom. The order of the rite as a whole, therefore, should be : a short admonition, the reading of the Epistle and Gospel in the vernacular, a homily, the marriage ceremony, the nuptial blessing.

(b) If there is no vernacular rendering of the Epistle and Gospel of the Mass for the bride and groom approved by the competent territorial ecclesiastical authority, a text approved by the local ordinary may be used for the time being.

---

16. During Lent and Advent the solemn celebration of marriage was forbidden, i.e. the celebration of marriage with nuptial Mass and nuptial blessing.

(c) There is no reason why there should not be chanting between the Epistle and Gospel. Similarly, the insertion of a 'prayer of the faithful' between the marriage ceremony and the nuptial blessing is much to be recommended. It should be in a form approved by the local ordinary and should contain prayers for the bride and groom.

(d) At the end of the ceremony a blessing should always be given to the bride and groom, even during the forbidden times, and even if one or both of the partners have already been married. The formula to be used is that found in the Roman Ritual, tit. VIII, c. 3, unless a particular national Ritual has a special blessing of its own.

75. If Matrimony is celebrated during the forbidden times, the parish priest should admonish the partners to take into account the special character of the liturgical season.

SACRAMENTALS   (Const., Art. 79)

76. In the blessing of candles on 2nd February, and of ashes on Ash Wednesday, only one of the prayers given in the Roman missal for these blessings may be used.

77. The blessings which are listed in the Roman Ritual, tit. IX, c. 9, 10, 11, and which up to now, have been reserved, may henceforth be given by any priest, except for the following : the blessing of bells for use in a church or an oratory (c. 9, n. 11), of the foundation stone of a church (c. 9, n. 16), of a new church or public oratory (c. 9, n. 17), of an antimension (c. 9, n. 21), of a new cemetery (c. 9, n. 22). Papal blessings are also excepted (c. 10, nn. 1-3), and the blessing and erection of the Stations of the Cross (c. 11, n. 1), which are reserved to the bishop.

CHAPTER FOUR:

THE DIVINE OFFICE

THE DIVINE OFFICE FOR THOSE BOUND TO CHORAL OFFICE   (Const., Art. 95)

78. Until such time as the reform of the Divine Office shall have been completed :

(a) Communities of canons, monks, nuns (monalium) and other regulars or religious who are bound to choir by canon law, or by their constitutions, must recite the entire office, over and above the conventual Mass, every day in choir.

Individual members of these communities who are in major

orders or solemnly professed – with the exception of lay brothers – must, even when they are legitimately dispensed from choir, recite alone the canonical hours which they have not said in choir.

(b) Cathedral or collegiate chapters must, over and above the conventual Mass, chant in choir those parts of the office to which they are bound by canon law or by particular law.

When an individual member of one of these chapters, therefore, is reciting office alone, he is bound to recite, over and above the canonical hours to which all clerics in major orders are bound (see Const., Art. 96 and 89), those hours to which his chapter is bound.

(c) In missionary regions, provided there is no infringement of the choral discipline of religious, nor of the law binding cathedral chapters, members of religious orders and members of chapters who are legitimately absent from choir by reason of the pastoral ministry, may avail of the concession granted in the *Motu Proprio, Sacram Liturgiam*, number 6, provided they have the permission of the local ordinary. The permission of the vicar general or of a delegate will not suffice, however.[17]

THE FACULTY OF DISPENSING FROM THE DIVINE OFFICE (Const., Art. 97)

79. The faculty, which has been given to all ordinaries, of dispensing their subjects, in individual cases and for a just cause, from the whole or part of the obligation to the Divine Office, or of exchanging it for another obligation, is extended to major superiors of non-exempt clerical institutes, and of societies of clerics who live in common without vows.

THE LITTLE OFFICES (Const., Art. 98)

80. No little office is to be regarded as having been drawn up after the pattern of the Divine Office unless it comprises psalms, readings, hymns and prayers, and unless it has some pattern of day-hours and is in some measure of conformity with the liturgical seasons (*quod . . . horarum diei necnon respectivi temporis liturgici aliquam rationem non habeat*).

81. For the time being, those little offices which have already been legitimately approved can be used in the Church's public

---

17. Article 6 of the *Motu Proprio* grants to Clerics not bound to choir the right to omit Prime and 'to chose among the remaining small hours the one that is most suitable to the time of day.'

worship, provided they have been drawn up according to the requirements outlined in number 80.

New little offices, however, require the approval of the Holy See before they can be used in the Church's public worship.

82. When the text of a little office is translated into the vernacular, with a view to using it in the Church's public worship, it must be approved by the competent territorial ecclesiastical authority, whose 'Acts' must be approved by the Holy See.

83. When there is question of granting permission to use a vernacular version of the little office to those who are obliged to it by their constitutions, or when there is question of dispensing them from their obligation or of changing it for another obligation, the competent authority is the individual subject's ordinary, or major superior.

RELIGIOUS AND CHORAL OFFICE   (Const., Art. 101)

84. The obligation, imposed by their constitutions on members of the states of perfection, of reciting in common the Divine Office or some little office, or some portions of them, does not hinder them from availing of the faculty of omitting Prime and of choosing from among the remaining small hours, the one that is most suitable to the time of day (*Motu Proprio, Sacram Liturgiam,* number 6).[18]

THE LANGUAGE TO BE USED IN THE DIVINE OFFICE   (Const., Art. 101)

85. Clerics are obliged to use Latin when reciting office in choir.

86. The faculty given to ordinaries of granting permission, in individual cases, to clerics to use the vernacular, when the use of Latin would constitute a grave impediment to the proper recitation

---

18 The Latin of this paragraph is as follows: ' Obligatio absolvendi in communi officium divinum, aut aliquem parvum Officium, aut eorum partes, sodalibus Statuum Perfectionis ab ipsorum Constitutionibus facta, facultatem non adimit omittendi Horam Primam, et ex ceteris Horis minoribus illam eligendi, quae diei momento magis congruat.'

Article 78 (a), it may be useful to point out, refers to religious who are bound by canon law or by their constitutions to recite the divine office *in choir.* It is these—canons, monks, moniales and religious bound to choral office—who may not avail of the concession granted by number 6 of the *Motu Proprio* even when they are legitimately absent from choir. The same people, however, may avail of it, for private recitation, on the missions when they are legitimately absent from choir because of pastoral duties (Article 78 (c).

of the office, is extended also to major superiors, both of non-exempt clerical institutes, and of clerical societies of common life, without vows.

87. When deciding whether, in an individual case, a grave impediment exists which would justify granting this concession one must take into account the physical, moral, intellectual and spiritual condition of the petitioner. However, in granting this faculty – which is granted solely in order to make the recitation of the Divine Office easier and more devotional – there is no intention of lessening the obligation to learn Latin, which is laid on all priests of the Latin rite.

88. In rites other than the Roman rite, the vernacular version of the Divine Office should be prepared and approved by the respective ordinary for that language-region. Where the rite has elements in common with the Roman rite, the version approved by the territorial ecclesiastical authority should be used. The whole should then be submitted to the Holy See for approval.

89. Breviaries for the use of clerics who have been granted permission to use the vernacular in the recitation of the Divine Office, in accordance with the Constitution, Article 101, §1, must have the Latin text as well as the vernacular version.

CHAPTER FIVE:

ON BUILDING CHURCHES AND

ALTARS FOR ACTIVE

PARTICIPATION

THE PLANNING OF CHURCHES

90. In erecting new churches, or in reconstructing or adapting existing churches, care should be taken that they be suitable for the performance of sacred actions, as befits their true nature, and for the promotion of the active participation of the faithful (see Const. Art. 124).

THE HIGH ALTAR

91. It is important that between the high altar and the wall of the church there be sufficient space to enable one to go right around the altar easily, and so that Mass facing the people can be celebrated on it. It should be so placed in the sacred building that, automatically, it becomes the true focus of attention for the entire congregation of the faithful.

In the selection of materials for building and ornamenting the altar, the prescriptions of the law are to be observed.

The sanctuary should be large enough to allow for the proper performance of the sacred ceremonies.

THE SEAT FOR THE CELEBRANT AND MINISTERS

92. A seat for the celebrant and ministers, which should harmonise with the structure of the church, should be so placed that it will be clearly visible by the faithful, and that the celebrant himself will be clearly seen to be presiding over the assembly.

At the same time, if the seat is placed behind the altar, it should not look like a throne, for this is reserved for the bishop alone.

SIDE ALTARS

93. Side altars should be few in number. In fact, if the building allows this, it is very fitting (*valde congruit*) to put them in chapels somewhat removed from the main part of the church.

ALTAR FURNISHINGS

94. The crucifix and the candles which are needed for the different liturgical actions can, if the local ordinary so judges, be put near the altar.[19]

THE RESERVATION OF THE EUCHARIST

95. The Blessed Sacrament is to be reserved in a solid, inviolable tabernacle, which should be placed in the middle of the high altar, or on a side altar which really stands out (*altaris minoris, sed vere praecellentis*). It may also, in accordance with the legitimate custom and in individual instances approved by the local ordinary, be placed in some other place in the church, provided it is really dignified and properly ornamented.[20]

It is permissable to say Mass facing the people even when there

---

19. The candles can be put on the altar steps, for example, on each side of the altar.

20. An example may be seen in the recently completed Church of St Colmcille, Tully, Galway, Ireland. The tabernacle is on a small shelf-like pedestal directly behind the high altar. Other solutions are the aumbry (tabernacle inserted in the wall) and the Gothic Sacrament-House (tabernacle on a pillar, which is frequently sculptured to suggest, for example, the tree of life). Germany provides examples of all three solutions. See Mr. Cantwell's detailed drawings.

is a tabernacle on the altar; it must, of course, be small, though suitable for its purpose.

THE AMBO

96. It is fitting to have an ambo, or ambos, for the sacred readings. They should be so placed that the ministers using them can be clearly seen and heard by the people.

THE CHOIR AND THE ORGAN

97. The choir and the organ should be so placed as to make it clear that the singers and the organist form part of the congregation, and to enable them to carry out their liturgical functions properly.

THE SPACE FOR THE FAITHFUL

98. The space for the faithful is to be planned with special care, so as to enable them to take part properly in the sacred actions, with eyes and heart. Normally, it is good to provide pews or seats, for their use. The custom of reserving seats for private individuals, however, is to be reprobated, in accordance with Article 32 of the Constitution.

Care should be taken that the faithful are not only able to see the celebrant and other ministers, but that, with the help of modern amplifying systems, they are able to hear them easily also.

THE BAPTISTERY

99. In the construction and ornamentation of baptisteries, great care should be taken to make the dignity of the Sacrament of Baptism clearly evident. Further, the space should be large enough to allow communal celebration (see Const., Art. 27).

His Eminence, Giacomo Cardinal Lercaro, transmitted this Instruction to His Holiness, Pope Paul VI. It had been prepared by the 'Consilium' for the Implementation of the Constitution on Sacred Liturgy, by command of His Holiness.

His Holiness examined the Instruction with all necessary care, being assisted in this both by the 'Consilium' and by the Sacred Congregation of Rites. On 26th September, in an audience granted to His Eminence Arcadio Maria Cardinal Larraona, the Prefect of the Sacred Congregation of Rites, he granted it his special approval, as a whole and in its parts, he confirmed it with his own authority, and ordered it to be published, and to be carefully observed by all concerned, as from 7th March 1965, the First Sunday of Lent.

Given at Rome, 26th September, 1964.

GIACOMO CARDINAL LERCARO
Archbishop of Bologna,
President of the ' Consilium ' for the Implementation
of the Constitution on Sacred Liturgy

ARCADIO M. CARDINAL LARRAONA
Prefect S.C.R.

✠ ENRICO DANTE
Archbishop tit. Carpathia
Secretary, S.C.R.

Bibliography

Papal Directives

Pope Pius XII, *Christian Worship*—Encyclical Letter *Mediator Dei*: C.T.S., London, 1954.

The Sacred Congregation of Rites: *Instruction on Sacred Music and Liturgy*. Issued 3 September, 1958. Translated by C. Howell, S.J.: *Sacred Music and Liturgy*. Herder, London. 1959. Pp. 62. 2/6. (This document is of vital importance for all that concerns Active Participation.) For a good, practical commentary, cf., J. B. O'Connell, *Sacred Music and Liturgy*. Burns and Oates. 1959. Pp. 112. 7/6. Far more satisfying, however, from a doctrinal point of view, is the French study, *Liturgie et Musique*, by A. G. Martimort and F. Picard. Paris: Les Éditions du Cerf. Pp. 230. 1959.

The General Decree *Novum Rubricarum* of July 1960. Translated (with Latin text) under title *The Rubrics of the Roman Breviary and Missal* by J. B. O'Connell. Burns and Oates, 1960. Pp. 202. For a practical commentary, cf *Handbook for the New Rubrics* by F. R. McManus. Chapman, London, 1961. Pp. 202. 21/-.

Books of Reference and Introductions

The most complete and accurate textbook is the monumental *L'Église en Prière*—Introduction à la Liturgie. Edited by A. G. Martimort. Desclée et Cie, Tournai (Belgique). 1961. Pp. 917. Less scientific but very complete and readable is W. J. O'Shea's, *The Worship of the*

Church—a Companion to Liturgical Studies. Darton, Longman and Todd, London. 1960. Pp. 582. Also very concise and reliable: J. A. Jungmann's *Public Worship.* Challoner, London. 1957. Pp. 249.

G. Lefebvre, *Catholic Liturgy.* Sands, London. 1954. Pp. 300. 12/6.

A.G. Martimort, *In Remembrance of Me.* Challoner, London, 1958. Pp. 217. 11/6.

I. H. Dalmais, *Introduction to the Liturgy.* G. Chapman, London, 1961. Pp. 208. 24/-. A fine theological synthesis, but rather too advanced for an Introduction.

Various Studies

Dom Lambert Beauduin, *Liturgy, the Life of the Church.* The Liturgical Press, Collegeville, Minnesota. 1926. Pp. 93.

Abbot Cabrol, *Liturgical Prayer, its History and Spirit.* Burns, Oates and Washbourne, London. 1922. Pp. 382. Also, by same author, *The Prayer of the Early Christians.* Burns, Oates and Washbourne. 1930. Pp. 174.

Romano Guardini, *Sacred Signs.* Sheed and Ward. 1937. Pp. 97. Also published by Pio Decimo Press, St. Louis 15, U.S.A. 1956. Another short work of this author now regarded as a classic: *The Spirit of the Liturgy.* Sheed and Ward. 1930. Pp. 149.

Dom Placid Murray, O.S.B., *Studies in Pastoral Liturgy I.* The Furrow Trust, Maynooth. 1961. Pp. 304. 12/6. This volume contains the papers read at the first five Liturgical Congresses at Glenstal. Volume 2 of this series, edited by Vincent Ryan, O.S.B. (The Furrow Trust—Gill and Son, 1963, pp. 314, 16/-) treats of *The Church and the Sick, Participating in the Mass, The Liturgy and Church Architecture.*

Charles Davis, *Liturgy and Doctrine.* Sheed and Ward. 1960. Pp. 100. 7/6.

E. Flicoteaux, *Our Lady in the Liturgy.* Challoner. 1959. Pp. 109. 7/6.

O. Rousseau, *The Progress of the Liturgy.* Newman Press, Westminster, Maryland. 1951. Pp. 219. This book treats of the history of the Liturgical Movement.

Dom Pierre Salmon, *The Breviary through the Ages.* The Liturgical Press, Collegeville, Minnesota, 1963. Pp. 175. $2.50.

V. Little, *The Sacrifice of Praise*—Introduction to the Meaning of the Divine Office. Longmans, Green and Co., London. Pp. 200. 10/6.

H. Tardif, *The Sacraments are Ours.* Challoner. 1956. Pp. 89. 8/6.

A.-M. Roguet, *The Sacraments, Signs of Life.* Blackfriars. 1954. Pp. 162.

Congress of the French C.P.L. held in 1955: *The Sacrament of Orders.* The Aquin Press, 1963. Pp. 358. 32/6. Presents a liturgical approach to the problem of "collegiality".

Mother Emmanuel Athill, *Teaching the Liturgy in Schools.* Challoner. 1958. Pp. 101. 6/6.

Lubienska de Lenval, *The Whole Man at Worship.* Chapman. 1961. Pp. 86. 10/6. A very valuable book from a catechetical point of view.

Godfrey Diekmann, *Come Let Us Worship.* Darton, Longman and Todd, London, 1960. Pp. 180. 21/-.

Gabriel Braso, *Liturgy and Spirituality*. The Liturgical Press, Minnesota, 1960. Pp. 247. $3.50 (about 24/6).

J. A. Jungmann, *The Early Liturgy up to the time of Gregory the Great*. Darton, Longman and Todd, 1960. Pp. 314. 50/-. A work of absorbing interest—opens a window on the early liturgical life of the Church. Equally valuable but rather too expensive: *Pastoral Liturgy*. Challoner, London, 1962. Pp. 430. 63/-.

Louis Bouyer, *Life and Liturgy*. Sheed and Ward, 1956. Pp. 284. 18/-.

Jean Daniélou. *The Bible and the Liturgy*. Darton, Longman and Todd, 1960. Pp. 372. 42/-. Excellent introduction to the symbolism of the liturgy.

Symposium, *The Liturgy and the Word of God*. Liturgical Press, Collegeville, Minnesota, 1959. Pp. 183. $3.50 (about 24/6).

I. H. Dalmais, *Eastern Liturgies*. Faith and Fact Series, Burns and Oates, 1960. 8/6.

Peter Hammond, *Liturgy and Architecture*. Barrie and Rockliff, London, 1960. Pp. 191. 37/6. Probably the best work of its kind. The author is an Anglican.

The Mass

J. A. Jungmann, *The Mass of the Roman Rite*. New Revised and Abridged Edition in one volume. Burns and Oates. 1959. Pp. 567. A veritable *Summa* of information on the prayers and rites of the Mass. Valuable as a work of reference. Two other short works by this author are of great interest: *The Sacrifice of the Church*. Challoner. 1958. Pp. 78. *The Eucharistic Prayer*—A Study of the Canon. Challoner. 1960. Pp. 55. 5/-.

Abbot Bernard Capelle, *A New Light on the Mass*. Clonmore and Reynolds. 1961. Pp. 66. A small masterpiece; cf. chapter on the meaning of the Offertory.

R. Guardini, *Before Mass*. Longmans, Green and Co. 1955. Pp. 203.

Pius Parsch, *Study the Mass*. Liturgical Press, Collegeville, Minnesota. 1953. Pp. 120.

A.-M. Roguet, *Holy Mass*—Approaches to the Mystery. Blackfriars, London. 1953. Pp. 120.

Dom Bede Lebbe, *The Mass*—an Historical Commentary. Browne and Nolan. 1947. Pp. 168. 8/6.

H. A. Reinhold, *Bringing the Mass to the People*. Burns and Oates, London, 1960. Pp. 114. 21/-. Contains many forthright proposals for a reform of the Mass-liturgy.

Mgr. Chevrot, *Our Mass*. Challoner, London, 1958. Pp. 241. 21/-.

William Barden, *What Happens at Mass*. Clonmore and Reynolds, Dublin, 1953. Pp. 111. A profound theological work with pastoral awareness.

Clifford Howell, *The Work of our Redemption*. The Catholic Social Guild, Oxford. 1962. Pp. 185. 6/-. At a popular level, first-class.

The Liturgical Year

Dom Guéranger's *The Liturgical Year* (8 volumes), although now rather dated, can be still read with profit.

The best complete commentary on the Liturgical Year now seems to be: Pius Parsch, *The Church's Year of Grace* (5 volumes). The Liturgical Press, St. John's Abbey, Collegeville, Minnesota. 1957. A more recent one-volume work draws on the liturgy of the feasts and seasons to illustrate the doctrine of grace—a boon to preachers: *Seasons of Grace*. Challoner, London, 1963. Pp. 369. 42/-.

Aemeliana Lohr, *The Mass Through the Year* (2 volumes). Longmans, Green and Co. 1958. *The Great Week* (A Commentary on Holy Week). Longmans, Green and Co. 1958. Pp. 208. 12/6. This is a very profound study—makes difficult but rewarding reading.

Louis Bouyer, *The Paschal Mystery*. Allen and Unwin. 1951. Pp. 347. This is now regarded as a classic.

Jean Gaillard, *Holy Week and Easter*. Liturgical Press, Minnesota, 1957. Pp. 172. 65 c.

Georges Chevrot, *On the Third Day: the Resurrection in the Gospel and in the Liturgy*. Scepter, Dublin 1961. Pp. 208. 16/-.

A. S. Burett, *We Celebrate Our Redemption*. Challoner. 1960. Pp. 77.

Dom Mark Tierney, *Holy Week—A Commentary*. Browne and Nolan. 1958. Pp. 103. Very practical for use in this country.

J. Lemarié, *La Manifestation du Seigneur* (A Study of Advent, Christmas and Epiphany). Éditions du Cerf, Paris. 1957. Pp. 537.

M. Premm, *The Year Made Holy*. Mercier Press. 1958. Pp. 198. 15/-.

A. M. Avril, *Preparing for Christmas*. Blackfriars. 1957. Pp. 153.

C. Howell, *Preparing for Easter*. Burns and Oates. 1957. Pp. 142. 7/6.

J. A. Jungmann, *The Meaning of Sunday*. Challoner, London, 1960. Pp. 32. 2/6.

Noële Denis-Boulet, *The Christian Calendar*. Faith and Fact series, Burns and Oates, 1960. 8/6. Very interesting on question of a fixed calendar.

E. Flicoteaux, *The Splendour of Pentecost*. Helicon Press, 1961. 35/-.

Periodicals

The Furrow and *Doctrine and Life* often publish articles of liturgical interest. The two following periodicals which are exclusively devoted to liturgical questions can be specially recommended: the American monthly review, *Worship*, published by the Liturgical Press, St. John's Abbey, Collegeville, Minnesota; the English review *Liturgy* (the quarterly of the Society of St. Gregory).

La Maison-Dieu is the organ of the French *Centre de Pastorale Liturgique*. Published quarterly (Ed. du Cerf, 29 Boulevard Latour-Maubourg, Paris 7e). An excellent scientific-pastoral review.

The Bible Today, the new American periodical (also published by the Liturgical Press), contains many items of liturgical interest. Appears six times yearly.

Liturgical Arts: An American quarterly published by the Liturgical Arts Society (7 East 42 Street, New York 17).

The Liturgy Constitution: editions and commentaries

Constitution on the Sacred Liturgy, Latin and English text, Liturgical Press, St John's Abbey, Collegeville, Minnesota, U.S.A.

Constitution on the Sacred Liturgy, English text in Father Clifford Howell's Translation, Whitegate Publications, 26a Castle Street, Cirencester, Glos., England.

Constitution on the Sacred Liturgy, a 'study-club' edition with twenty-page commentary by Gerard S. Sloyan, the Paulist Press, New York.

The Church's Worship: Considerations on the Liturgical Constitution of the Second Vatican Council, by J. D. Chrichton, Geoffrey Chapman, London.

Vatican II: La Liturgie, French translation of Constitution and *Motu Proprio*, with directives of French Hierarchy and introduction by Bishop Henri Jenny, Editions du Centurion, Paris.

La Maison Dieu: text in Latin and French in No 76, full-scale and valuable commentary in No 77, by Fathers Roguet, Gy, Jounel, Gelineau and Seumois, Editions du Cerf, 29 Boulevard Latour-Maubourg, Paris 7, France.

Implementation of the Liturgy Constitution

Many of the national hierarchies of the world have finished work on their programmes for the implementation of the Constitution on the Sacred Liturgy. In accordance with the *Motu Proprio*, Sacram Liturgiam, these programmes and the vernacular renderings of the liturgy have been submitted to the Council for the Implementation of the Constitution on the Sacred Liturgy. The council (*consilium*) is presided over by Cardinal Giacomo Lercaro and its secretary is Father Annibale Bugnini, c.m. Its forty-two members represent twenty-seven nations.

We publish here the two most recent statements issued by the Irish hierarchy and by the hierarchy of England and Wales on the implementation of the Constitution.

ENGLAND AND WALES

The following is the full text of the Instruction issued at the beginning of November 1964:

The publication of the long-awaited *Instructio ad Exsecutionem Constitutionis de Sacra Liturgia Recte Ordinandam* makes it possible at last to give guidance with regard to the celebration of Mass in the presence of a congregation of people, and with regard to administration of sacraments and other blessings in English.

The official translation of the entire *Instructio* is being prepared and will be published for the hierarchy by the Catholic Truth Society with the least possible delay.

Although the *Instructio* does not take full effect until the first Sunday of Lent 1965, the changes mentioned in this letter (being directly connected with the decree authorized by the hierarchy and approved by the Holy See), together with the English text issued last August by the hierarchy for use at Low Mass, will take effect from the first Sunday of Advent this year.

In view of differing circumstances in various parts of the country, each Ordinary will inform his clergy of the days and conditions when the various changes in the Liturgy are to be regarded as obligatory and when they are merely permissive.

A study of the complete text of the *Instructio* will reveal changes in other liturgical matters not mentioned in this letter. Further direction concerning these will be issued in due time. Similarly, it will be appreciated that it is not possible to implement immediately the use of English in certain parts of the proper of the Mass (even where permission from the Holy See has already been obtained) until a worthy translation has been prepared. A committee is already at work on the translation of those parts of existing liturgical books for which permission to use English has been granted. It is hoped that the text of an officially-approved Missal for Sundays and greater festivals will be published next year.

A. USE OF ENGLISH AT LOW MASS

1. The vernacular may be used for the prayers at the foot of the altar, i.e., the Sign of the Cross, *Confiteor*, *Misereatur*, *Indulgentiam*, and the remaining versicles and responses; the *Gloria in Excelsis*; *Dominus vobiscum*; the Epistle (and other Lessons when they occur) and Gospel, together with the versicles and responses which precede and follow them; the Creed; *Orate Fratres* and *Suscipiat*; the *Pater Noster*; *Ecce Agnus Dei*, the triple *Domine non sum dignus* and the *Corpus Christi* (all at the people's Communion); and, at a Requiem Mass, the *Requiescant in pace. Amen.*

2. For the readings from Scripture, the following versions are approved: Douai, Knox, Confraternity of Christian Doctrine and, in Wales, the Welsh version.

3. For other parts of the Mass where the vernacular is to be used an approved English text for use at Low Mass has been made available to all Catholic publishers from whom suitable cards for use by the people have been prepared. It is hoped that altar cards, etc., for use by the priests will shortly be available.

(Please note that the *Kyrie eleison*, etc., is to be recited in Greek. The *Pater Noster* may be recited in English. These changes have been made since the official text was issued.)

B. GENERAL REGULATIONS

The following directives concerning the celebration of Low, Sung or High Mass are to be observed throughout England and Wales as from the first Sunday of Advent:

1. Psalm 42 and its antiphon are always to be omitted from the prayers at the foot of the altar.

2. Whenever Mass is preceded by any other liturgical function (e.g., *Asperges*, blessing of candles, etc.), all prayers at the foot of the altar are omitted and Mass begins at the Introit.

3. Those parts of the proper or Ordinary of the Mass which are recited by the people, or sung by the people or the choir, or read by a Lector, are not recited privately by the celebrant.

4. All kissing of the hand and of things given to or received from the celebrant is to be omitted.

5. For the public reading of the Scriptures at Mass, editions of books suitable for use in the sanctuary, e.g. pulpit editions of the Epistles and Gospels, are to be used.

6. The Epistle and Gospel (and other Lessons when they occur) are to be read or sung facing the people.

7. Throughout the doxology which ends the Canon (*per ipsum . . . per omnia saecula saeculorum*) the celebrant holds the chalice and Host slightly raised over the altar, omitting all signs of the Cross. He holds them thus until the people's *Amen*, when he replaces them upon the altar, and only after this does he genuflect.

8. At the people's Communion the *Ecce Agnus Dei* and the triple *Domine non sum dignus* are always to be said in the vernacular. The celebrant no longer makes the sign of the Cross with the Host giving Holy Communion to others. As he says the words 'The Body of Christ', he holds the Host raised a little above the ciborium for the communicant to see before saying 'Amen'.

9. The Last Gospel and the Leonine Prayers are always to be omitted. The customary regulation for the prayer for the Queen remains in force.

C. LOW MASS

1. When the celebrant comes to the foot of the altar, all make the sign of the Cross, saying: 'In the name of the Father and of the Son and of the Holy Ghost. Amen'. Then the celebrant crosses himself again, saying: 'Our help is in the name of the Lord', to which the people reply: 'Who made heaven and earth'. He then recites the *Confiteor* in English and all continues as indicated on the cards bearing the officially-approved text.

2. The Epistle and any other Lesson (and the Gradual, etc., which follows) may be read to the people by a Lector or by one of the servers. Until an officially-approved English version has been prepared, the Gradual, etc., must still be read in Latin. The Gospel may be proclaimed only by a priest or deacon.

3. Before reading the Epistle (or Lesson) the priest or Lector says: 'The Epistle/Lesson appointed to be read today is taken from . . .'. When he has concluded the reading he bows to the book of Sacred Scriptures and the people answer 'Thanks be to God'.

4. If the celebrant himself is to read the Epistle and Gospel, he either stands at the altar facing the people or goes to an ambo (or lectern) or to the altar rails, as may be convenient. If either or both are to be read by someone other than the celebrant, the reading must be made from an ambo (or lectern) or at the altar rails.

5. If the celebrant himself is to read both Epistle and Gospel from an ambo (or lectern) or from the altar rails, he turns towards the altar while reciting *Munda cor meum*; if he is reading them from the altar (facing the people) he bows in the centre before the altar as in the present rite.

6. If the celebrant is to read only the Gospel he goes to the sedilia after the Collect(s) as at High Mass. He rises during the recitation of the Gradual, etc., after the Epistle, and goes to stand before the altar on the floor of the sanctuary; he bows deeply while reciting *Munda co-meum* and then goes to the place from which the Gospel is to be proclaimed.

7. If the celebrant is to read neither Epistle nor Gospel, he goes to the sedilia after the Collect(s), as at High Mass. He blesses the priest or deacon who is to proclaim the Gospel, and afterwards the Book of Gospels is brought to him to kiss.

8. If a deacon or priest other than the celebrant is to proclaim the Gospel he recites the *Munda cor meum* and is blessed by the celebrant as at High Mass. After reading the Gospel, he brings the book to the sedilia for the celebrant to kiss.

9. The following parts of the Mass are to be said aloud by the celebrant: (a) the Secret; (b) the doxology at the end of the Canon (*per ipsum . . . per omnia saecula saeculorum*); (c) the Embolism (the prayer *Libera nos* which follows the *Pater Noster*).

10. The *Pater Noster* may be recited in English by celebrant and people together, up to and including 'Amen'.

D. HIGH MASS

The celebrant and his ministers bow to the Choir only at the beginning and end of the ceremony.

1. For the *Kyrie, Gloria, Sanctus-Benedictus* and *Agnus Dei* the celebrant remains at the altar and sings these parts of the Mass with the people. Clearly this does not apply in the case of polyphonic Masses.

2. The Epistle and Gospel are to be sung in Latin. They may subsequently be read in English in the customary way immediately before the homily.

3. The Epistle and Gospel are to be sung from an ambo (or lectern) or from the altar rails. For the Epistle, the subdeacon may either hold the book or have it on a lectern; but the Book of Gospels must always be enthroned on a suitable lectern, the sub-deacon standing beside the deacon during the singing of the Gospel.

4. The celebrant sits during the (Lessons and) Epistle. He remains seated to bless the subdeacon after the Epistle and to put in and bless the incense; but he rises to bless the deacon. He remains at the sedilia for the Gospel (after which the Book of Gospels is brought to him to kiss) and for the *Credo* (if there is one), not returning to the altar until it is time to sing *Dominus vobiscum* before the Offertory.

5. The paten is no longer held by the subdeacon after the Offertory but is left on the altar. The subdeacon wears the humeral veil to bring the chalice, etc., to the altar. Then he returns to the credence where the veil is removed and he takes up his usual place at the foot of the altar.

6. The following parts of the Mass are to be sung by the celebrant: (a) the Secret—the same chant as for the Collect is to be used; (b) the doxology at the end of the Canon—until new music is provided, a monotone is to be used; (c) the Embolism—until new music is provided, a monotone is to be used.

7. The people may join the celebrant in singing the *Pater Noster* in Latin (up to and including *Amen*), using the ordinary tone given in the Missal.

E. SUNG MASS

1. For the *Kyrie*, *Gloria*, *Credo*, *Sanctus-Benedictus* and *Agnus Dei*, the celebrant remains at the altar and sings these parts of the Mass with the people. This does not apply in the case of polyphonic Masses.

2. The Epistle and Gospel may be read in English instead of being sung in Latin; where this occurs, the preceding versicle and response and the final response are said in English.

3. Regulations 2, 3, 4, 5, 6, 7 and 8 for Low Mass apply also to Sung Mass.

4. When the celebrant himself proclaims the Gospel using incense, he must do so from the ambo (or lectern) or from the altar rails and not from the altar unless he is facing the people.

5. Regulations 6 and 7 for High Mass apply also to Sung Mass.

F. SACRAMENTS

1. The use of English in the administration of the sacraments, as set out in the latest edition of the *Small Ritual*, also comes into effect on the first Sunday of Advent. Only this version may be used. With regard to the sacrament of Penance, the local Ordinary will instruct his clergy as to the use of the vernacular. Confessors are reminded that the reference to excommunication, suspension and interdict may be omitted from the form of absolution where there is no serious likelihood of their having been incurred. This is important in the confessions of children whose minds can only be confused by the mention of them.

IRELAND

The following is the full text of the statement issued on 8 November 1964 by Most Rev. Dr. Conway, Archbishop of Armagh and Primate of All Ireland, from the Irish College in Rome. It was issued on behalf of the Hierarchy:

The Irish Hierarchy is happy to announce that the Holy See has approved, by a decree of 4 November 1964, the decisions made by the bishops regarding the introduction of the vernacular, Irish and English, into certain parts of the Mass.

In accordance with the wishes of the Holy See the changes will be introduced in several stages in order to achieve as smooth a transition as possible in the ceremonies of this central act of Catholic worship.

The bishops are taking immediate steps to have printed texts of the approved translations available for priests and people so as to permit the introduction of the first stage, where feasible, on the first Sunday of Lent, 1965, when the important stages in the ceremonies of the Mass, recently announced by the Holy See, will come into effect.

In addition to the Epistles and Gospels, translations have been approved for the prayers said at the foot of the altar at the beginning of Mass, for the *Kyrie, Gloria, Credo, Orate Fratres, Sanctus, Pater Noster, Agnus Dei* and the *Ecce Agnus Dei* and *Domine Non Sum Dignus* before the people's communions. Translations of certain other parts of the Mass will be submitted for approval in due course.

Announcements as to the implementation of the changes in each diocese will be made by the ordinary of the diocese.

The bishops are introducing these changes in the conviction that they will help to strengthen and deepen the great traditional devotion of the Irish people to the Holy Sacrifice of the Mass, and they are confident that all, priests and people, will do their utmost to ensure that they achieve this purpose. The Second Vatican Council, speaking of the Sacrifice of the Mass – 'by which the Sacrifice of the Cross is perpetuated through the centuries' — says 'The Church earnestly desires that the faithful, when present at this mystery of faith, should not be there as strangers or silent spectators, but should through a proper understanding of the ceremonies and prayers take part in the sacred actions, conscious of what they are doing with their devotion and collaboration'. At a later stage it is hoped to have translations approved for a more extensive use of the vernacular in the sacraments and sacramentals and particularly in the funeral services.

Application

of the directives of the Instructio to the

Design of Churches and Altars

WILFRID CANTWELL, B.Arch., F.R.I.A.I.,
F.R.I.B.A.

The following illustrations are put forward as possible solutions to the problems posed by the directives given in Chapter V of the Instruction of the Sacred Congregation of Rites for the proper implementation of the Constitution on the Sacred Liturgy. The illustrations are diagrammatic and will require to be adapted to suit the particular requirements of each church. The comments given with the illustrations are those of the author and are not claimed to be authoritative. It should be kept in mind that the directives are not complete and that further decisions by the Commission may involve modifications of the solutions suggested in the following pages; consequently a flexible approach to actual design problems should be adopted as far as may be possible.

ELEVATION

PLAN

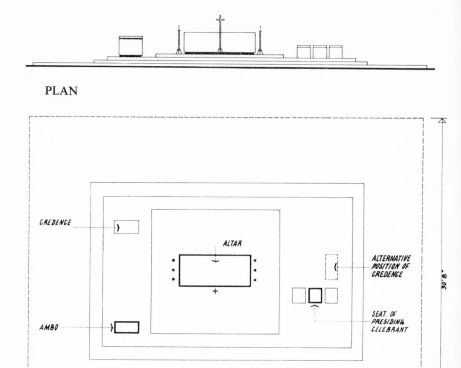

The central place of the altar should not be interpreted as the geometrical centre of the building, i.e. a circular or square church with seats on all sides of the altar, as this can result in an excessively formal concentration which encourages an individualistic approach to the liturgy and detracts from the essential community spirit. The central space should rather be thought of as the centre of gravity, i.e. that point towards which, by common impulse, the congregation naturally tends. This latter concept leaves a wide freedom in the development of appropriate architectural ideas and of plan shapes.

Two features of the Sanctuary are to be given a new or, in some cases, an additional importance. The seat for the celebrant is no longer to be merely a convenient and, often, insignificant chair but it is now to be, in an obvious manner, the seat of the president of the congregation and it must be, therefore, dignified although not ostentatious in design. The celebrant will occupy this seat for a considerable proportion of the time of the liturgical functions and his seat should be located so that it will be clearly visible by all of the congregation. The second distinctive feature, the ambo, is considered on page 155.

LAYOUT OF SANTUARY AREA FOR A SMALL PARISH CHURCH

ELEVATION

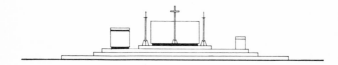

PLAN

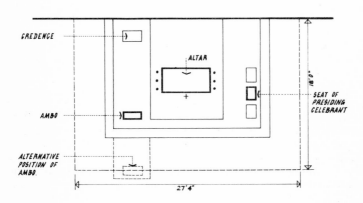

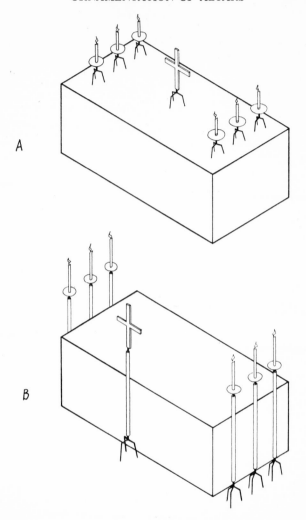

A. Where the cross and candlesticks are placed on the altar they must be small and light in appearance in order not to obstruct the view of the celebrant; on a large altar this could result in a mean and insignificant effect.

   B. Where it is permitted by the ordinary, placing the cross and candlesticks on the predella beside the altar can make a more dignified treatment of these items possible and, at the same time, can indicate more clearly the essential nature of the altar.

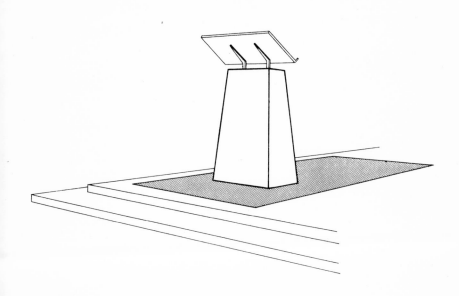

The ambo must not appear, from its location, size or appearance, to resemble a pulpit. It is essentially a lectern or reading desk and it should not be excessively prominent. As the 'Place of the Word' it is however next in importance to the altar in the sanctuary and its treatment should be dignified; any decoration would be based most appropriately on some theme of the Gospel. The ambo should have its own distinctive place (a simple change of floor treatment would, normally, be sufficient definition) but, as the readings are an integral part of the liturgy it must not be divorced from the altar and, therefore, its location should be reasonably close to the altar which it should resemble, also, in its materials and general form.

1. The customary position for the tabernacle is on the main altar. This is the least satisfactory place as it involves a dichotomy of symbolism between the sacrificial offering on the altar and the simultaneous Real Presence in the tabernacle. It also involves an inevitable obstruction of the view of the celebrant's actions by the congregation.

2. The problem of sight lines can be solved by the use of special 'effects' (e.g. partially-sunken tabernacles) but these give a demeaning appearance which is inappropriate. A less eccentric solution is the construction of a two-level altar with the tabernacle on the lower level; this, however, is restrictive of access to the main altar and, unless it is very carefully handled, can make the tabernacle appear to be merely an appendage to the altar.

3. With the approval of the ordinary the tabernacle could be placed in a suitably-decorated shrine which should be in a prominent part of the church. This arrangement could be acceptable in a small church but in a large or even in a medium-sized church it would be extremely difficult to avoid an apparent relative insignificance in its siting.

4. The special communion table, provided that its form does not lead to confusion with the sacrificial altar, is a dignified and very practical location for the tabernacle. Care must be taken to ensure that the siting and detail design does not distract from the altar.

5. The best solution to the problem of siting the tabernacle is to place it as an aumbry in the wall of a side chapel and behind the altar. Such a chapel would be eminently suited to private devotion and could be used for services when the congregation is small.

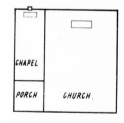

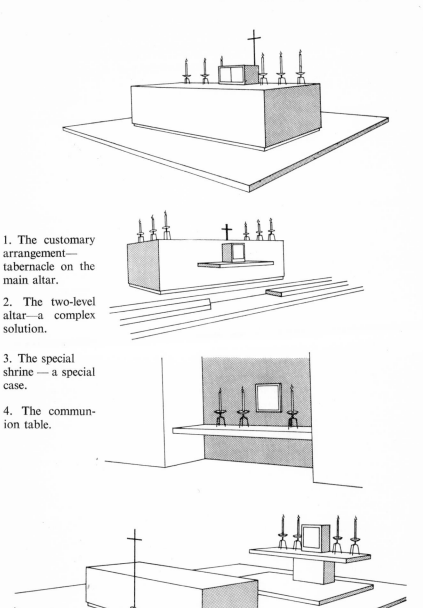

1. The customary arrangement—tabernacle on the main altar.

2. The two-level altar—a complex solution.

3. The special shrine — a special case.

4. The communion table.

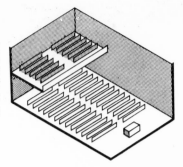

The primary function of the choir is to *lead* the congregation in the singing and responses of the liturgy. It cannot do this if it is isolated from the congregation (e.g. in a gallery or behind a screen) as it then becomes a performance listened to but not joined in by the people.

Nevertheless the choir should have its own distinctive place not only because this is necessary in order to ensure uniformity and cohesion in the signing but also as an indication of the leading position which it occupies in the congregation.

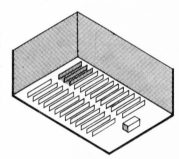

The most effective position, acoustically, for the choir in the majority of cases will probably be at the rere of the congregation but this also has the disadvantage that the choir may not appear to be a part of the congregation and that there may be difficulty in co-ordinating the choir, organist and celebrant.

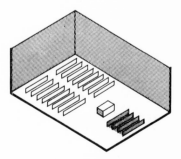

Behind the altar and facing the congregation will, usually, be the next most effective position acoustically but it has the disadvantage of separating the choir and congregation excessively in a very small church.

Immediately in front of the congregation provides the maximum integration of choir and congregation but with the less active congregations it could result in the establishment of a barrier between sanctuary and people.

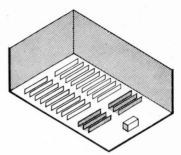

To one side of the sanctuary is probably the best position for the choir as it can still appear as part of the congregation, even if a special part, and it does not set up any barrier and it has the advantages of facilitating co-ordination and of dialogue between choir and congregation.

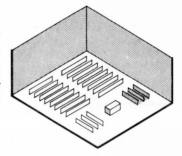

The organ must not be placed either too close to or too far from the choir as the balance and rhythm of sound can be disturbed (a musical expert and organ builder should be consulted in the initial stages of the building design). The only other restriction on the location of the organ is that it should not be placed where it is liable, because of its size and striking form, to distract attention from the more important features of the church.

The organist and his console must be very close to the choir. The organist must be able to supervise completely both the choir and the sanctuary area but he should not be too close to or easily visible by the congregation.

Active participation by the people in the liturgy requires not only good acoustics and good sight lines but also physical proximity to the centre of activity, the altar. If any of these requirements is missing the individual will, inevitably, feel isolated and will tend to withdraw into private prayer rather than to unite with his brothers in the social worship of God.

The requirements for good acoustics are complex but the main one is that the size of the church should be kept as small as possible; if any seat is more than 80 feet from the altar it will be extremely difficult to provide tolerable acoustics—the long narrow church is, therefore, unsuitable.

Good sight lines can be obtained only by a theatrical raking or stepping of the floor for seats more than 60 feet from the altar and such a treatment would tend to encourage a false 'spectator' attitude.

Long Church

Physical proximity can be achieved most fully with a strictly centralized plan but only at the expense of establishing so strong a radial line from altar to person that the community sense can be lost.

The ideal church plan, therefore, will normally be relatively small in area—not more than about 6,400 sq. ft. for the sanctuary and seating area—with no predominant axis and with some degree of freedom in its layout.

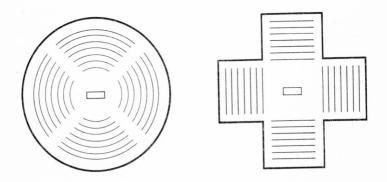

Centralized Churches

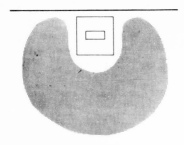

natural unrestrained pattern
of assembly.

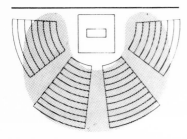

rigid geometric translation of
natural group.

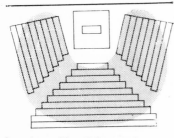

freer but still radial grouping.

Seating of any kind, unless very carefully handled, can have undesirable effects:

(a) it can create a sense of emptiness and of isolation when the church is only partly filled with people;
(b) it can establish barriers between the people and the altar by setting up rigid physical lines of obstuction;
(c) it can impose a formal layout which implies a relationship of person to altar only and not of person to person as well with the result that the communal aspect of worship may not be fully realized;
(d) it can encourage a 'spectator' attitude in the congregation as the seated area appears to be the 'public' part of the building and the sanctuary to be the 'performing' part which the congregation merely observes.

Active participation by the people in the liturgy should make most people willing to do without seats for the short period of the liturgy so that only a few seats for the aged and infirm would be necessary, but this attitude is not likely to develop very quickly.

As seating will, usually, be required its undesirable effects can be mitigated by:
(a) relating the seating to the floor as much as possible, i.e. the floor should be dark in colour and have a strong texture or pattern while the seats should be light in colour and as low as possible (an arm-rest height

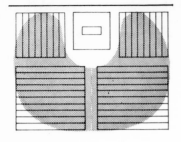

of 2 feet 2 inches is recommended);

(b) using interlocking, stacking chairs instead of benches as more flexible and more adjustable layouts can be obtained and the congregation is less rigidly enclosed in a wooden framework.

relatively informal and more satisfactory layout.

THE BAPTISTERY

Baptism is a public sacrament, the entry of an individual into the community of the Church, and therefore it should be celebrated in the presence of the Church which is the congregation and, ideally, immediately before the principal parish Mass on Sundays.

Baptism requires a defined space not only architecturally but also sacramentally; the baptistery is a holy place just as is the altar (the place of Sacrifice) and the ambo (the place of the Word).

The form and setting of the baptistery should, in itself, represent the sacrament (the baptistery is not intended merely to *serve* liturgy but to *be* liturgy) and it should, by its location and design, remind each member of the congregation of his own consecration to God.

The baptistery should not be placed in a confined or remote position (e.g. in the base of a tower or in a small side chapel) nor should it consist only of an isolated font, no matter where located or how beautifully designed, as community participation becomes impossible in a restricted space and the dignity of the sacrament is minimized by the absence of an adequate setting.

A baptistery in a completely separate building, as was common in European churches, would require to be almost as large as the church in order to make community participation genuinely possible and it would rarely be practicable because of cost. It is further undesirable because it tends to divorce the regenerating action of baptism from its proper consequence—the reception of the Eucharist.

The baptistery can be attached to the main body of the church by placing it in the entrance porch which, however, should be fairly open to the church if the congregation is to be able to participate.

Placing the font to one side of the porch (1) tends to relegate it to a relatively unimportant position.

It is more in keeping with the vital nature of the sacrament to place the baptistery just inside the main entrance (2) and with adequate planning it should not obstruct circulation in such a position.

Providing a large atrium (3) distinct from the porch, although expensive, is a still better solution as it will encourage the congregation to gather around the font for the baptism before entering the Eucharistic room.

A more economical method of achieving the advantages of the atrium layout is the integrated plan in which the font is brought into the Eucharistic room. The best way of doing this is to provide a large open space (4) at the rere of the church in which the baptistery is located. This arrangement retains the symbolism of baptism as the entry to the church and the congregation can still assemble around the font.

If cost considerations dictate a minimum of free space the baptistery can be placed slightly to one side (5) and the congregation can still, though less easily, join in the service from their seats.

Placing the font near the sanctuary (6) gives the congregation the best physical conditions when the space is very limited but it has the disadvantage of suggesting that baptism is not a *prior* necessity for *admittance* to the Eucharist at the altar.

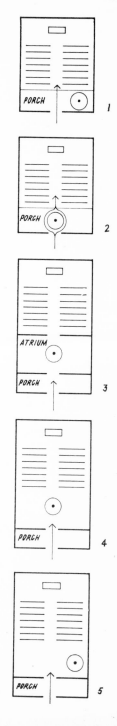